Endorsements

This book le... the ... practice of knowle... straightforward answ... ... ticular, change management is ... ...ue for knowledge managers and this is cover... ... ...y each step of the way. Many organizations are making pr...gress in putting elements of knowledge management into place. However, significant performance improvements come from synergistic effects when initiatives reinforce and support each other. Chris Collison and Geoff Parcell are immensely practical in their approach to KM, yet manage to communicate a clear vision of 'the big picture' – of how an integrated approach can impact business performance. This second edition of their book is enriched by a wide variety of case studies showing how KM is making a difference in private, public and not-for-profit organizations.

Dr Christine van Winkelen, Director,
Henley Knowledge Management Forum

'Sharing best practice, continuous improvement, a culture of learning and measuring our progress ... these are just some of the ways that Learning to Fly *has influenced NHS thinking and practice. I am sure this work will continue to make an important contribution to how we make the most of "what we know" as we continue to improve services for patients and staff.'*

Professor Helen Bevan,
Director for Innovation and Knowledge,
NHS Modernisation Agency.

'For companies like ours, whose strategy is based on sharing knowledge and best practice, this book provides practical advice about how to put these words and good intentions into action. The challenges can be substantial but the rewards equally so for the companies that get it right. Knowledge management is critical to staying ahead in today's ever-changing and competitive marketplace. Chris Collison and Geoff Parcell do a fantastic job of sharing their insights about how best to make this happen.'

Sir Roy Gardner, Chief Executive, Centrica plc.

'The first generation of knowledge management has come and gone. The second generation, which promises both deeper insights and greater impact, will be less about data and more about the social nature of knowledge, less about "capture and retrieval" and more about innovating and sharing, and ultimately more about know-how rather than know about

- the only knowledge that ultimately matters in any pragmatic institution.

BP's dramatic ascent as an industry leader stems in no small part from its commitment to learning and knowledge. Chris Collison and Geoff Parcell show how new ideas and tools are making working and learning inseparable in one of the world's most innovative large companies.'

Peter Senge, Senior Lecturer, MIT and Chair,
SOL (Society for Organizational Learning)

'Collison and Parcell compellingly demonstrate how the combination of sharing behaviors, smart processes and enabling technology have made BP a world leader in knowledge management.'

Steve Ballmer, President and Chief Executive Officer,
Microsoft Corporation

'There are very few knowledge management books written by actual practitioners and this is one of them. BP has led the charge in KM and these authors were there. A fine place to start one's KM education!'

Larry Prusak, Executive Director,
IBM Institute for Knowledge Management.

'In the last five years few companies have implemented their knowledge management strategy as effectively as BP. Chris Collison and Geoff Parcell have used this compelling experience to provide a thoughtful and action-oriented guide to knowledge management. It should be required reading for both students, practitioners and, perhaps most important, for those executives that have to deliver on the promise of leveraging knowledge assets as a mechanism for gaining competitive advantage.

Dr. John C. Henderson, Richard C. Shipley
Professor of Management, Boston University

'A great story of a global company on the journey toward the Knowledge Driven World. From building networks across the organization to "having the time to halve the time" it is a journey of constant change for the better.'

Robert H Buckman, Chairman and CEO,
Buckman Laboratories

'Finally in the jungle of theoretical sources about knowledge management, a really practical, "hands-on" book which gives useful insights in the practice: How to initiate knowledge management and even more important how to keep it alive – as normal part of everyday business.'

Cordula Söfftge, BMW Group Learning Concepts

Chris Collison is an internationally recognised consultant, author and speaker in the field of knowledge management and organisational learning. After 15 years in corporate roles, Chris now works as an independent consultant and professional advisor. Chris was at the heart of BP's pioneering work in knowledge management for many years, before moving to Centrica as Director of Change and Knowledge Management. His clients include Orange, Freshfields Bruckhaus Deringer, Oracle, ConocoPhillips and Nationwide together with a number of national and regional Government departments. He combines his track record as a practitioner and his experience in practical, real-world knowledge management with an ability to inspire at board level. Chris is an associate at Henley Management College and a Chartered Fellow of the CIPD.

See www.chriscollison.com for further details.

Geoff Parcell is a master practitioner of knowledge management and a business coach. As a core member of BP's knowledge management team, Geoff helped deliver significant business value. He was profoundly moved by an 18 month secondment to the UN helping share good practices on responding to HIV and AIDS and is now available as an independent consultant sharing his know-how with a variety of private and public sector organisations. He now supports multi-cultural groups to learn and share what they know and turn that knowledge into action. He helps groups to embrace change, move ideas to wide-scale implementation and nurture effective communities of practice. He remains connected with the response to AIDS and is a director of the Constellation for AIDS Competence.

See www.practicalKM.com for further details.

Geoff and Chris work together building organizational capability in knowledge management through a variety of workshops and masterclasses.

See http://www.learning-to-fly.org for details.

CAPSTONE
be inspired!

Capstone Publishing (A Wiley Company)
John Wiley & Sons Ltd
The Atrium, Southern Gate
Chichester, West Sussex PO19 8SQ

Tel: +44(0) 1243 779777
Fax: +44(0) 1243 770638

Learning to Fly

'Deliver more, and do it with fewer resources.'

Isn't that the productivity challenge that everyone in business is facing today? A key way to achieve this is by sharing know-how. That is, by using and adapting what someone else has already learned. Many people know instinctively they should be doing this, but struggle to know how to get started.

Today, no one is, nor can be, an expert in everything. In every challenge, it is easy to feel that you don't know enough to keep up with the accelerating pace of change inside your organization, let alone the world outside. Start with the assumption that somebody somewhere has already done what you are trying to do. How can you find out whom, and learn from them?

This significantly updated and enhanced edition of Learning to Fly shows exactly how to put knowledge management theory into practice, sharing the tools and insights of two leading practitioners.

In Learning to Fly, Chris Collison and Geoff Parcell share their experiences from a wide range of the world's leading and learning knowledge management organizations. It is a practical, pragmatic workbook packed with hints and tips to help managers put knowledge management into action immediately. This edition also comes with a supporting CD-Rom with many useful and intelligent interactive tools for the budding knowledge manager.

Geoff and Chris work together building organizational capability in knowledge management through a variety of workshops and masterclasses. See http://www.learning-to-fly.org for details.

£19.99/US $19.95/Cn $28.99

Learning to Fly

Practical knowledge
management from some of
the world's leading learning
organizations

Chris Collison and Geoff Parcell

CAPSTONE

The right of Chris Collison and Geoff Parcell to be identified as the authors of this book has been asserted in accordance with the Copyright, Designs and Patents Act 1988

First edition published 2001
This edition published 2004 by
Capstone Publishing Limited (a Wiley Company)
The Atrium
Southern Gate
Chichester
West Sussex
PO19 8SQ
www.wileyeurope.com
E-mail (for orders and customer service enquiries): cs-books@wiley.co.uk

Reprinted April 2005, September 2006, February 2007, December 2007, March 2009, March 2010, November 2011, February 2013

CIP catalogue records for this book are available from the British Library and the US Library of Congress

ISBN 13: 978-1-84112-509-1 (PB)

Typeset in Trebuchet by Sparks Computer Solutions Ltd, Oxford (www.sparks.co.uk)

This book is dedicated to:

Stella, Chris and Bronwyn

Louise, Martha and Hannah

Contents

was the difference and why was it different? What can we learn from that?

What has happened since the publication of the first edition, what went well, and what would we have done differently?

N o one can tell the story of what a company does, and its character better than the people who work for it.

Over the last few years BP has grown, organically and through mergers and combinations, and is now one of the largest companies in the oil and gas industry. Size alone, of course, means nothing. Size didn't save the dinosaur.

The potential value of size, which is there for us to capture, is the knowledge held by 100,000 of the world's brightest people. Knowledge of a particular technology, a relationship, a way of doing business, which has been proved successful. The value comes from sharing that knowledge and applying it in different places and different situations.

This collection of real-life stories describes a company that is just beginning to learn how to learn, and people who are just starting to share the knowledge.

People like Morton Haga, an engineer from Norway who realised he was using a combination of drilling tools in an unusual way, and achieving a dramatic improvement in performance by so doing. An improvement worth around $300,000. He put his ideas on the BP intranet, and the very next day they were read by his colleagues in Trinidad who were able to use them to achieve comparable gains.

People like Fumu Mondoloka, our marketing manager in Cape Town, who asked for help from a marketing network that stretches across the company, and who received by return ideas from the team in Aberdeen, which made possible a breakthrough in his thinking and made it possible for him to secure a significant new deal, selling lubricants in Tanzania.

I hope this book will inspire others to achieve similar sharing of knowledge - within BP and beyond. Just imagine what we could achieve if we all knew what each one of us knows.

John Browne
Group Chief Executive, BP
January 2001

'Deliver more, and do it with less resources.'

Isn't that the productivity challenge that everyone in business is facing today?

A key way to achieve this is by sharing know-how – by using and adapting what someone else has already learned. Many people know instinctively they should be doing this, but struggle to know how to get started.

'How can I know enough not to be foolish - or to be fooled by someone else?'

Today, no one is, nor can be, an expert in everything. In every challenge, it is easy to feel that you don't know enough to keep up with the accelerating pace of change inside our organizations, let alone the world outside.

Start with the assumption that somebody somewhere has already done what you are trying to do. How can you find out whom, and learn from them?

You can read any number of excellent books on the theory of knowledge management. This one demonstrates how to put theory into practice, starting with the tools used and the experience and insights gained of two leading practitioners working within BP, and adding the insights and experiences from practitioners in other organizations.

So why are two people who worked for BP writing this book? We felt that it is a story worth telling. We have learned a lot through our journey of discovery and continue to do so, in different environments. We want to share some of what we have learned with you, and we want to stimulate you to learn and apply what you have learned in order to become ever more productive. We have written half of the chapters each, which may account for any slight differences in style and stories. The book tells of our experience of knowledge management, the tools and techniques we have found useful, what we have done to create the right environment and how it has evolved. In this new edition, we have added a series of stories and examples from other organizations. The stories have been offered to us by people from a diverse group of 'leading and learning' organizations, ranging from the BBC to the United Nations; from De Beers diamond mines in Botswana to Noumea Primary School in New South Wales. It is their diversity and their desire to share which has enriched this edition of the book, and enhanced the tools and processes that we described in the original version.

It is still a practical, pragmatic workbook *full* of hints and tips to help people make their very next steps.

You won't find too much theory here. Rather it is a book about what we have practised and what we have learned from practising it. We are writing it in our 'spare time' because we are busy putting knowledge management into action. It is the story of how we originally applied it within BP, one of the world's largest organizations, and then pushed the boundaries further in new environments. By comparing this with your own experiences, in your own context, we know you will be able to adapt what you do to be more effective. We have seen these tools and techniques applied in a variety of businesses - large and small. Others have applied them successfully in different organizations - charities, government organizations and other business sectors. We know that the principles, the model and the tools are scalable and transferable, because readers of the book and members of the 'Learning to Fly' community have told us of their successes. But don't take our, or their word for it. Read on!

The book has been laid out in a style to emulate Web pages in order to make it easier for the reader to focus on what they want to know, rather than what we, the authors want to tell them. There are links between pages so if you are following a certain line of thinking you can follow that directly to relevant knowledge. Alternatively the book can be read conventionally. The chapters include facilitator's notes, and action zones highlighted by the following icon:

How can you get the best out of this book?

At the action zones, pause in your learning and start doing something applicable to your own situation.

In the new edition we have included a CD containing a collection of links, slides, presentation materials, summaries, video clips, examples and tools. We have referenced these throughout the book with the following icon:

- Part I of the book provides an overview. It sets the context, defines knowledge management, provides a model to use and describes the environment for successful knowledge management. In short, it provides the basis to get started.

- Part II of the book describes how we have applied a number of tools and techniques to help us manage knowledge. They help us learn before, during and after everything we do. They help us get in touch with people who know, and to develop communities who act as guardians of the company's knowledge.

- Part III looks at how we are embedding the principles within company-wide processes and where we aim to go next.

- At the back we've included some resources to help you get started.

Read the chapters relevant to you, draw comparisons with your own experience and do something different. Then reflect and learn from what you have done. If someone comes to us and says 'I read your book and applied some of the ideas. This is how my business has improved as a consequence,' then we will know that the time spent preparing the original, and this new version of the book has been worthwhile.

So whether you want to know what knowledge management is about, wonder how to take the important next steps, or just want to hear how different organizations have successfully applied it, this book will appeal to you.

It is a book for the businessperson, the business student, the public servant, the educationalist, and information professional. It is a book for the generalist business person as well as specialists working in the field of knowledge management.

Finally, this is a record of what we know at a single point in time – now. Our world continues to change, and we continue to learn. We look forward to hearing what you learn through the experience of reading, and most importantly *applying*, what follows in this book.

Acknowledgements

While exploring knowledge management, we have learned a lot. We have learned from a great range of people both inside and outside BP, too many to mention, in some cases too many to remember, and in a few cases too many to be aware of. We have learned from people in our businesses applying the principles, tools and techniques in their own context, and generating the stories and quotes that you will find throughout the book. It is only because many people have *really applied* knowledge management in BP, that we were motivated to write this book. Theory doesn't excite us, but business results, as a consequence of the application of knowledge management, do.

We will single out BP's Knowledge Management Team led by Kent Greenes, with whom we laughed, cried and learned much together. This team worked tirelessly for two years to fan flames, and light new fires across the company – fires that have spread and are still burning brightly today. The other team members were Neil Ashton, Catherine Day, Gareth Edwards, Tony Kuhel, Nick Milton, Walt Palen, Keith Pearse, Barry Smale, Dave Wolstenholme and Tom Young.

Additionally, we wish to recognize the Drilling Learning Team for their early pioneering work in knowledge management, and more recently, the Operations Excellence Team, who have embedded knowledge sharing into the daily business of thousands of operations staff.

We are grateful to Barry Smale and Phil Forth for their thoroughness in critiquing the book in its draft form, and for providing their suggestions for improvement so rapidly.

Finally, we are indebted to our wives, Louise and Stella for supporting, encouraging, sacrificing, reviewing, challenging, uplifting and at times, gently deflating our egos!

Chris Collison and Geoff Parcell, September 2000

Since working beyond the boundaries of BP, we have learned a lot more. We have seen the tools and techniques that we used in one of the world's largest companies applied in very different contexts – in the United Nations UNAIDS programme and in Centrica, a large international energy and essential services company, headquartered in the UK. We have discovered what we took for granted in BP, and learned how to develop knowledge-sharing cultures in very different environments – with different starting points and different outcomes. Without question, we still have more to learn.

As the subtitle suggests, this edition of *Learning to Fly* is far more than a revision. In the original, we told the story of BP's knowledge management journey, and set out the tools and techniques that made that journey such a success. Four years on, hundreds of organizations have made their own journeys, and a number of those 'leading and learning' organizations have volunteered to share their experiences with us, and become a part of the ongoing story. *Thank you.*

Specifically, we are grateful to:

Our former colleague, Nick Milton, now at Knoco Ltd, Astrid Foxen from Tearfund, Giles Grant and Ken Brierley from BNFL, Ian Corbett from De Beers, Jenny Lewis at Noumea Primary School, Andrea Vowles, Sandra Lowe and Emily Jacob at Centrica, Dr Jean Louis Lamboray and Marlou de Rouw from UNITAR, Tony Pilgrim, Clare Chaundy and Euan Semple from the BBC, Lucy Lamoureux from KM4DEV, Patrice Jackson at SAIC, Jorden

Hagenbeek at Squarewise and the 500 members of the 'Learning to Fly' community who continue to encourage, support, challenge and further develop the tools, techniques and stories that we have shared.

Finally, we are now even further indebted to our wives, Louise and Stella who foolishly believed us when we said that the first edition would be the last. At least they'll know better next time ...

Chris Collison and Geoff Parcell, June 2004

Part I
Overview

Setting the Context

Chapter One

Have a read of this chapter to set the context for the rest of the book.

In it we describe what each chapter is about in order to help you navigate your way around. So whether you want to get an overview of knowledge management, or whether you want some tools or techniques that you can apply, or want to know what BP and many other organizations are currently doing with KM, you'll learn exactly where to go.

'Ve just finished dealing with a kitchen design engineer. I want to improve my kitchen layout. We spend a lot of time in the kitchen and although its functional, it could be turned into something altogether more efficient and with a better ambience. So I have called in an expert. How can I ascertain whether this person knows what they are talking about, and whether what they are proposing is absolutely necessary, fits our body shapes and is in my interest rather than merely lining the pockets of the engineer?

How do you trust an expert?

The simple answer is I can't, I have to trust my expert. But how can I trust an engineer that only crossed my threshold 15 minutes ago? I can begin by asking a few simple questions and listen to the responses I get; not only to the content of the responses but also the way he delivers them. Is he talking down to me, or talking in technical terms and acronyms that I don't understand? Or is he pitching it at a level I can understand and checking for my understanding? Is he telling me stories to demonstrate a point and at the same time demonstrating his track record?

> *'I did a job for a television presenter in Maidenhead recently and she had a built in microwave, a fridge with slide out drawers and a fantastic cooking hob in the round. She was ecstatic, not only was preparing quick meals for the family simplified, she could also entertain dinner guests in the kitchen whilst she was finishing the cooking. And do you know what her favourite dish was?'*

What of his appearance? He is dressed smartly to show some respect, but has hands that are clearly used to manual work. He has the tools of his trade about him, a measure, a pencil and pad, and a screwdriver to prod at the plaster. What does that tell me about the quality of the job he is likely to do?

This is the third engineer I've invited round to quote. We looked for a selection from the *Yellow Pages* telephone directory, all work locally and each offers something different. As well as being able to compare the prices for the job, I am learning better questions to ask and also what differentiates their service and their products. Now which one shall I choose?

Increasingly each of us is being asked to be accountable for more and more both at work and in our private lives. Who suffers if the kitchen is not installed properly? I do. We have to keep out of the kitchen for a while longer and my family complains to me. We learn all the time; *we learn what questions to ask so that when the time is right we make the right decision.*

Start by asking simple questions

The authors got started in knowledge management by asking simple questions of others both inside and outside their organization, BP. As they developed confidence in themselves and inspired confidence in others that they could make a difference, they had a real impact on business performance. Once you have sorted out what you know and what you need to know, it's easy to ask a question to fill the gap in your knowledge.

BP is a multinational company of 100,000 people involved in:

- exploration for, and production of, oil and gas;

- refining of crude oil;

- the marketing of gasoline, lubricants and aviation fuel;

- the manufacture and sales of petro-chemicals;

- gas production, distribution and sales;

- power generation; and

- solar power.

BP is also socially and environmentally responsible and makes money for its shareholders. BP is headed by Lord Browne, who believes that sharing what we know drives improved business performance. The company is divided into 150 businesses, some with as few as 50 people. We have learned that the principles of knowledge management can be adapted to any size of business.

One of the first projects we worked on was in Vietnam. BP has a business there developing a project to produce gas from the South China Sea, and deliver it onshore where it is converted to electricity to support the country's growing power requirements. The business had been made aware of knowledge management at a time when negotiations with the Vietnamese government had broken down, and they were prepared to try anything once.

'What is the main issue you have to deal with?'

We flew in to Ho Chi Minh City with Ed Guthrie, a retired US Army Colonel, without any clear idea of the problem or of how we might solve it. And we were the experts!

We asked a simple question, 'What is the main issue you have to deal with?' We asked that of a large number of people in the organization for the first three days. There were different views on what the issue was, each person seeing the issue from their own particular stance. By reviewing the responses we got we were able to pose more focused questions to understand the issues better. Ed noticed the parallels between the US Army's approach and BP's approach to Vietnam.

'You came here for one reason, looking for a big oilfield. Yet when you found something different, gas, you didn't change your tactics, your approach. You wanted the Vietnamese to follow your way of doing business. That's just like us (the US Army). We came into this country, in the '60s for one reason. What we found was rather different. They didn't operate to our rules.'

Adapt good practices into your own context

This is where transferring best practice comes unstuck so often. Rarely can something that has worked well in one location and in one situation be applied directly to another. The solution often disappoints. In this book we'll share with you some real examples and expect you to consider whether they are useful for you to adapt into your own context. We've always struggled with who it is that can define good practice. We believe it is the person who uses the practice that next determines whether it makes a difference to what it is they are doing.

Getting started ... you are already doing it!

Many books have been written on the subject of knowledge management. We have presented to many businesses on the topic. Yet often people come along and say 'Now what do I have to do to actually get started?' Let me tell you the first secret ... you are already doing it! In fact, it's more difficult not to do it. Each of us has everyday encounters where we want to find out something extra from someone who knows more. 'What's the best way of getting a train into London?' 'If I'm thinking of going to Disney World in April what is the best option?' I'm going to get a new kitchen fitted? What are the things I need to know about? What have I forgotten?

In today's world, getting into action fast gives us a sense of progress, but if it's the wrong task or a task done in the wrong order, we may be wasting our resources doing the wrong thing.

Learning before, learning during and learning after

Far better then to do the research before you start, talk to people who have already done it or had it done. Pause too at regular intervals to reflect on what has happened so far and how that might modify what you do in future. At the end, take time to review what was actually achieved versus what you had planned for at the outset. Learning before, learning during and learning after is a key principle of knowledge management. Taking the time to learn in order to make the time to do will lead to better results.

Just think for a moment about the last time you purchased, leased or ordered a car. Did you spare it much thought? Or did you go to the first

Like the time you bought a car

car dealer and select one? Each of us has a different preferred buying strategy. I spend time doing some research for mine. My preferences may have been triggered by an advertisement in a magazine or on TV. I may have admired a friend's or colleague's car; even had a ride in it one lunchtime. Can you recall how you started?

I then read reviews and comparisons in car magazines. For me this is the fun part, looking at a spreadsheet of criteria that compares the acceleration from 0–60mph, the engine size, and the storage capacity in cubic litres. I then visit a few showrooms to stroke the bodywork, feel the seats and test-drive a limited number of models. I adjust the driver's seat and steering wheel to my satisfaction; listen to the sound of the engine accelerating, and block out the sales patter of the over-eager salesman. I then go away to think about it for a while, talk it through with my loved one, and ask advice from colleagues driving a similar car, perhaps ask a mechanic. But what finally convinces me?

> *Stop here* and think about how you went about your last car purchase. How did you choose what you bought? And what finally convinced you to part with your money or signature?

Now, how often do you put that much effort into making a business decision at work?

What is this book about?

What we describe in this book is a model for the environments we work within. It is a model that can be applicable to any organization. We talk about tools that we have found useful, and we think you will too. We also talk about our view of where we are heading with knowledge management. We have laid out the book in a style to emulate Web pages in order to make it easier for you to navigate directly to the areas that you want to know about. We've made links between pages, so if you are following a certain line of thinking you can continue directly to relevant knowledge. Alternatively, the book can be read conventionally from start to finish.

Navigating through the book

Would a bit more detail help you decide where to start? Whatever size of organization you are in, you will find it useful. OK, here are the fourteen chapters again with a paragraph about each. The first five provide an overview. The next seven describe practical tools and techniques. Then there is a chapter describing where BP currently is in applying these tools and techniques to drive business performance. Finally we review, in order to know better next time.

1 *Setting the Context*. This describes what the book is about and how it is set out to enable you to navigate the knowledge quickly.

2 *What is Knowledge Management?* Knowledge management has proven very difficult to define. It is about capturing, creating, distilling, sharing and using know-how. That know-how includes explicit and tacit knowledge. Know-how is used as shorthand for know-how, know-what, know-who, know-why and know-when. It's not about books of wisdom and best practices, its more about the communities that keep know-how of a topic alive by sharing what they know, building on it and adapting it to their own use. It is not a snapshot of what is known at a single point in time, but an evolving set of know-how kept current by people who regularly use it.

What is knowledge management?

3 *The Holistic Model – It's More Than the Sum of the Parts*. To make a real difference in delivering results through sharing know-how, it is important to work every element of a process model. The model describes how to turn business objectives into results by learning before, learning during and learning after. It also requires tapping into and feeding the know-how of the community and network and recognizing that knowledge is more than a book of wisdom of best practices.

Apply it holistically

By applying the model consistently and persistently the authors know business results will improve.

4 *Getting the Environment Right*. One of the most difficult things to do in today's business environment appears to be to request help. People fear that requesting help is an acknowledgement that the requestor is not up to the task. Setting the environment up so that it is OK to ask for some assistance from peers is key. Inside BP there is no doubt that one big enabler was to create an infrastructure of common machines and versions of software networked across the globe. This offered the potential to share, but did not guarantee the

Ask for help

delivery of the business results. Getting the right processes and the right leadership in place, and accessing the people with the right behaviours was key to delivery.

5   *Getting Started – Just Do It.* Understanding what knowledge management is about intellectually is a first

Ask a simple question   step. Understanding that the model has several components, each of which must be worked on, is helpful. Procrastinating takes it no further. We learned to get started by just working on something simple. It could be as simple as asking a question – 'What is the key issue for this business?' – then listening carefully to, collecting and distilling, the responses to play back. As long as there are regular reviews to check and adjust your activity, the shared learning will begin at once.

That sets the scene. Now let's look at some of those tools and techniques.

6   *Connecting Sharers with Learners – Using Self-Assessment.* One of the barriers to sharing and learning is

Connecting sharers with learners   a perception that 'we're different'. Another is a sense that someone else is dictating the agenda for knowledge sharing. We discovered a way to create a common language, which is the basis for sharing. Through self-assessment, groups set their own priorities, and then find the right people to share with, and learn from, in a kind of informal benchmarking where everybody has something to contribute, and something to gain. We brought all this together through a neat visualization that we called the 'river diagram'. This river has flowed around the world – in the fight against HIV and AIDS, driving operational excellence in BP and improving customer management in Centrica. It's also a great way to get focused and get started.

7   *Learning From Your Peers – Somebody Has Already Done It.* Peer Assists are a technique to learn early on

Learn before   in the 'doing' phase – a kind of project-design meeting if you like. It's about sharing what people know in their own context, then sharing this with others who share what they know in their context. By knowing what is generic, and what the differences are, it enables people to create future possibilities together, which can be firmed into options and then action. Learning is not complete until a different action has been taken as a consequence.

8 *Learning Whilst Doing - Time to Reflect.* Learn during
A technique learned from the US Army is called After Action Review (AAR). As well as quickly learning from the last event, so that it can be applied to the next, it is also a means of building a stronger team. It is simple to do, flexible, and when applied consistently, effective. In the US Army they do it anywhere - including on the back of a truck after a skirmish with the enemy!

9 *Learning After Doing - When it's All Over.* Learn after
At the end of a project, or distinct change, sit down with all the people who have a stake in the result, and review what went well and what could have been done differently. Consider who can benefit from what has been learned. Identify a customer for the knowledge. Recount specific examples and focus on the activity rather than imply blame. Consider what you would do differently if you were to do it over again. Ask the customer what they have learned from this review; their insights may well be different, as they have a different set of experiences to filter the messages through.

10 *Finding the Right People - If Only I Knew* Get hold of the people
Who. Key to learning what others have who know
done is to know who to ask, and being able to reach them easily. Know-how is organically held by the community or network and constantly reused, revised, adapted and distilled. Key to knowing who, and being able to reach them, is a yellow pages or index of people's skills, experiences and contact details.

11 *Networking and Communities of Practice*. People with common interests or discipline practices frequently form networks, or communities of practice, to share their know-how, either to improve the capability of each individual to do his or her job better, or to deliver on a common goal or objective. These networks sometimes meet face-to-face but more often make use of a multitude of technology aids to collaborate virtually.

Become a node on the network

12 *Leveraging What We Have Learned – Capturing Knowledge.* It is important to find a way of capturing what has been learned, in order that others can reuse it, sometimes immediately and otherwise after a distinct time lag. It is important to identify a customer for this captured knowledge or it is unlikely ever to be used again.

Capture and share good practices

What gets captured first is the practices, sometimes these are shared and can be called common practices. What makes a good practice though and who can decide what is good? And how can we speed up the process of identifying the good practices?

13 *Embedding it in the Organization – Preparing to Let Go.* You know when sharing knowledge has become an unconscious competence, when there are no longer people dedicated to knowledge management in the organization, when the techniques are embedded in the core business processes. At BP, the focus has been on embedding them in company-wide, operational excellence processes, and in sharing project lessons to enhance capital productivity. People who are already busy no longer have to think about learning before, learning during and learning after. It is embedded in the way they do things.

Make it an unconscious competence

The next phase includes identifying the other core processes and embedding the tools of learning before, during, and after into them.

14 *Review of the Book – What Did We Set Out* | Apply what we have
    To Do? This chapter applies one of the key | learned
    tools outlined in the book: the Retrospect.
    Let's review what we set out to do, what
    did we actually achieve? Why was there a difference and
    what can we learn from that? Our intent was to write a
    book that is both practical and pragmatic, to help people
    take their first steps to do something different in order
    that they can learn from that and adapt further. And then
    to learn from *their* experiences. Did we achieve that and,
    if not, what was the difference and why was it different?
    What can we learn from that?

So spend a few moments writing down three questions that occur to you. Having read this chapter
what do you most want to know next?

1 _____

   _____

   _____

2 _____

   _____

   _____

3 _____

   _____

   _____

Bon Vol!

In this chapter:

• Defining knowledge management – what it is, and what it isn't.

• Creating the environment.

• Components of knowledge management.

• Not just know-how but also know-why, know-who, know-when, know-what and know-where.

• Tacit versus explicit knowledge.

• From unconscious incompetence to unconscious competence.

'What did you do at work today, Daddy?'

How do I answer Hannah, our three-year-old daughter, in a meaningful way? How do I summarize the manner in which I spend my day trying to align and simplify corporate activities, investigating collaborative technologies, encouraging people to capture and share lessons learned, facilitating discussions in networks, matchmaking between different parts of our business, developing intellectual capital strategy ...

Explaining knowledge management in simple terms

'Um.' (Thinks … How can I make this sound interesting?) *'I talked with some people on the telephone, sent some e-mails, read some stories on the computer, had some sandwiches, sent some more e-mails, helped some people to make friends with some other people and then came home to you and Mummy'* (Did that sound interesting?)
'What sandwiches did you have?' (Clearly not!)

Whether to peers at the office, close friends or inquisitive children, knowledge management has never been particularly easy to describe, define or explain. It's not a great topic for parties either, in case you've ever tried!

Defining knowledge management

One of our favourite definitions comes from Arian Ward, of Work Frontiers International:

> *'It's not about creating an encyclopaedia that captures everything that anybody ever knew. Rather, it's about keeping track of those who know the recipe, and nurturing the culture and the technology that will get them talking.'*

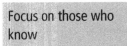
Focus on those who know

This shifts the emphasis from the creation of vast knowledge repositories, and places the higher value on the knowledge in people's heads and finding ways to increase its mobility.

- Have you ever had the feeling that someone just must have done this before, but you don't know who or where to find him or her?

- Have you ever had a chance encounter at the water cooler and learned a piece of information just in time to influence what you were doing?

We have.

Larry Prusak of IBM speaks of a continuum of knowledge ranging from 'capture' at one end to 'connectivity' at the other.

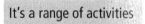

Capture   Connectivity

A focus on capture drives a set of activities relating to codification and procedures for knowledge. Organizations such as the US Army serve as good examples of this approach, investing large efforts in creating and distributing explicit knowledge – information packs, briefing notes and knowledge bases, and Web sites – all with tremendous efficiency.

An alternative approach is to invest time and energy in the processes and technologies that stimulate connections between people. This could involve the creation of communities and networks, peer interactions, collaboration tools and knowledge directories. These connections and conversations in turn address the transfer of tacit knowledge – the knowledge locked up in the heads of individuals that tends not ever to be written down, but flows between staff sharing war stories at a bar, or when one member of staff is mentored by another.

It's a range of activities

These two extremes illustrate the range of options available. Neither one is right or wrong; the selection of a point on the spectrum should simply be a reflection of the culture in an organization at a point in time. Some point on that spectrum represents the best return on your KM investment.

> Take a minute or two to consider this. Where is the largest prize for your organization? At which point on the spectrum should you invest your effort?

BP's position has been biased towards the 'connectivity' end of the spectrum, although some focused knowledge capture also formed an important part of our approach.

Tacit versus explicit

It's in people's heads

Knowledge can be held in people's heads (we call this tacit knowledge) or it can be written down (explicit knowledge). It is not possible to capture the full richness of what's in people's heads. If you don't believe us, try writing down your knowledge of how to ride a bicycle!

... and it's written down

On the other hand, explicit knowledge can be stored and searched, and can be a good catalyst for connecting people together. Then, questioning can bring out the tacit knowledge.

A way of thinking about capture and connectivity is to consider the relationship between 'what do others know' and 'what is known'.

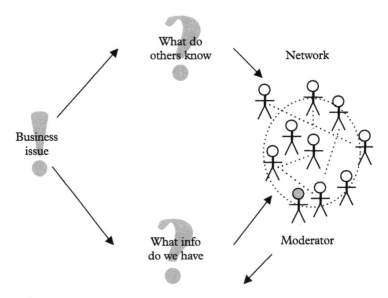

Think about one of your important business issues – perhaps it's a need to expand sales, recruit the right people or retain customers.

As you think about this issue, there will be two routes that you might take in seeking out knowledge.

- One is looking for *'what do others know,'* and searching them out and talking with them directly – this often leads to a network of other leads and contacts, or a community of practice.

- Another is to seek out *'what is known'* – what has already been captured or written down as information that I could make use of?

The weakness of the second approach for us has been that once captured, knowledge grows stale unless there is some mechanism for refreshing <mark>It needs refreshing</mark> it. Some would go further and maintain that a document cannot contain knowledge but only information. The information triggers thoughts, which you compare with your memory of past experiences; or it connects you with others. This in turn enables understanding.

Our experience is that to be useful knowledge needs to be refreshed frequently and it takes the organic nature of a network to own and refresh it with new experiences.

Perhaps this is why companies that sell mineral water market their products as 'natural spring water' and 'bottled directly at the source.' When was the last time you bought mineral water that was 'drawn from the lake?'

In the diagram above, the mechanism for refreshing 'what is known' is where the moderator of the network takes responsibility for maintaining and updating the body of knowledge – closing the loop.

A hybrid science – or is it an art?

Knowledge management is a hybrid discipline, neither art nor

Get a balance of people, process and technology

science; functionally it can straddle the fields of learning and organizational development, human resources and IT. This overlap is often represented as three circles. Knowledge management is the area where the three circles overlap.

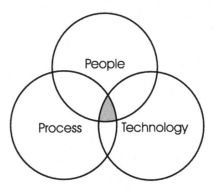

The messages in this model are powerful. The elements for successful knowledge management include:

- a common, reliable *technology* infrastructure to facilitate sharing,

- connecting the *people* who know, and the behaviours to ask, listen and share, and

- some *processes* to simplify sharing, validation, distillation.

All too often we embark on a change programme, and concentrate energy disproportionately on one, or possibly two of the circles. If we focus on people and technology, but neglect to consider process, then we risk automating the past.

Technology and process together are powerful partners, but without the people aspect, there is a strong risk that any effort to make change will generate resistance.

Finally, by considering people and process, but neglecting technology, we fail to capitalize on the power that IT brings to make explicit knowledge globally accessible, and, through multimedia and video-conferencing, to make tacit knowledge more widely available.

The activities of managing knowledge

There is a large marketplace for knowledge management products and techniques; your in-tray and inbox are probably full of flyers and advertisements for them. Software companies will sell you the latest collaboration and search tools, consultancies will sell you learning processes, and journalists will sell you their services for capturing corporate history.

Whilst these components can all be valuable in isolation, we believe that the greatest value is generated when these pieces of the puzzle come together in a complementary way. *If you know the picture that you are trying to create, it is easier to spot the gaps.* Knowledge can be created, discovered, captured, shared, distilled, validated, transferred, adopted, adapted and applied.

Create, discover, capture

Adapt, adopt, transfer, apply

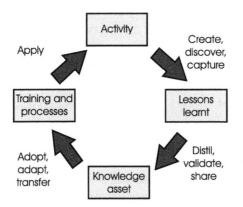

Starting with a business activity, the first step is to use a learning process to reflect on what happened, and draw out the lessons learned. Whilst it is great to capture lessons, a huge database of these can

Distil, validate, share

become wearisome to navigate. Our experience was that finding a way to distil the key points from these lessons and capturing them as a more concentrated 'knowledge asset' was far more helpful for people.

However, there's no guarantee that people will actually refer to these, unless there is some way of transferring and embedding these key learning points into the training materials and business processes that staff use. Then the knowledge actually becomes applied, and something changes.

Let's face it - if nothing changes, then knowledge management is unlikely to impact your bottom line.

What do we mean when we talk about knowledge?

OK, so if defining knowledge management is difficult maybe defining knowledge is more straightforward?

It is very common to see a blurring of the meaning of data, information and knowledge. Over recent years, databases have been re-cast as more fashionable 'knowledge bases' in order to appeal to the marketplace. They are closely related and we have found it useful to make some distinctions.

When I travel to Boston I get the following *data* from our travel office on an e-mail: AA79 21st August Dep: 13:45 Arr: 15:30. Fine. But in order to get there I could use a bit more *information*. The plane leaves from Terminal 4 at Heathrow and there is a business-class lounge that I can use. By talking with some colleagues who travel to Boston regularly I *know* that it is possible to request an upgrade to first class, that I can use a fast track through customs and that the plane generally arrives ahead of schedule.

Knowledge is richer than data or information

The knowledge I now have is related to the data but much richer and enables me to make some decisions. Of course I have to trust those colleagues in order to put some confidence in their knowledge.

The Concise Oxford Dictionary defines knowledge as 'familiarity gained by experience.' Sometimes we need to experience it ourselves to know. At other times it is sufficient that someone else, who has experienced it, shares that experience with us. Whether or not you act, based on someone else's experience, will depend on how well you know and trust them.

People sometimes interchange the terms 'know-how' and 'knowledge,' but there is a danger that in doing so we miss some other important attributes of what could be considered as knowledge.

Know-how is the processes, procedures, techniques and tools you use to get something done.

> It's more than know-how – its know-why, know-what, know-who, know-where, and know-when

Know-why relates to strategic insight – understanding the context of your role, and the value of your actions. It's the 'big picture' view of things. Think back to your first ever job. Did anyone explain to you why what you did was important, or were you just expected to 'get on with it' and not ask stupid questions? Know-why is a key to lifting morale and generating commitment from staff.

Know-what is the facts required to complete a task, it's the information needed in order to take a decision and it's the things you need to collect together before making something.

Know-who includes knowledge about relationships, contacts, networks, who to call on for help. It's the 'I know a man who can' factor. All of us apply and build up this type of knowledge on a day-to-day basis, often subconsciously. If your role is sales-oriented, you'll know just how important know-who can be.

Know-where is that uncanny ability that some people have for navigating through and finding the right information. You probably know people in your office who fulfil this role, functioning like human search engines. If you visit Yahoo!, or one of the other major Internet portals, you'll be in a knowledge-rich environment where most of the content is know-where – links to where relevant know-how can be found on the Internet.

Know-when is the sense of timing – to know the best time to do something, to make a decision, or to stop something.

Is 'knowledge management' the best label?

Choosing the best words to describe what you do

Despite the term being something of an oxymoron, we used the term 'knowledge management' to describe the area in which we were working. Some people have taken issue with us over the term and somehow feel threatened by our control of their knowledge. 'Performance through learning,' 'organizational learning,' 'shared learning,' 'knowledge sharing' or simply 'working smarter' could be used. It's worth investing time up front with people from your organization to select the most appropriate term. The wrong words could get in the way.

Creating the environment

It's like herding cats

I once heard knowledge management likened to herding cats. Stop for a minute and imagine yourself in a large room – or even a field – full of cats, trying to herd them towards one corner.

Not going well, is it? So if you can't *herd* cats, how could you get them to do what you want? You might suggest providing scratching-posts, saucers of milk, warm fires and balls of wool – components that go to make up the right environment.

... so get the environment right

That's exactly the view we took when thinking about knowledge management. You can't manage knowledge – nobody can. What you can do is to manage the environment in which knowledge can be created, discovered, captured, shared, distilled, validated, transferred, adopted, adapted and applied.

In order to create an environment within which knowledge rapidly flourishes we need:

- *the right conditions*: a common reliable infrastructure and an organization willing to be entrepreneurial;

- *the right means*: a common model, tools and processes;

- *the right actions*: where people instinctively seek, share and use knowledge; and

- *the right leadership*: where learning and sharing is expected and role-modelled.

Knowledge management as an unconscious competence

If you go into the rest rooms in many of BP's offices and look in the mirror you'll see a sticker that reads, 'You are looking at your Safety Officer.' It makes a good point. We have worked many years to embed the concept of safety management into the workforce – to spread the message that safety is everyone's responsibility, not just the responsibility of your manager or a central function.

Sustainable knowledge management

Knowledge management can be approached in a similar way – the ideal outcome is that people manage knowledge as part of their daily business without thinking of it as an extra task, and that the leadership of the company and the company processes reinforce this.

The following four steps illustrate this point.

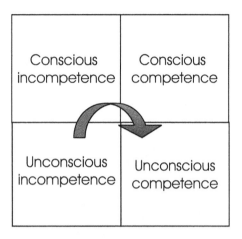

Start at the bottom left corner – *unconscious incompetence.* This first box is the 'ignorance is bliss' section. Perhaps as an organization, you aren't good at managing knowledge, but it has never occurred to you that it was a problem, or that this is something that should concern you.

My wife Louise taught me to drive when we'd been going out together for about six months. When I started driving, I had a bad habit of 'grating the gears,' but I was oblivious to that fact – unconsciously incompetent.

Moving to the next step, this is when light dawns – as an organization, you become aware that you are failing to manage knowledge effectively, and that you need to take action. This is *conscious incompetence.*

'Do you know that you always do that?' Louise said to me during driving lesson number three. 'You always grate the gears. You keep missing third.' Once my fragile ego had recovered, and I'd finished blaming the gearbox, I had to admit that she was right. I'd become consciously incompetent – progress!

The third step is where you deliberately focus your efforts. Having identified a gap in your capability as a company, you implement a programme, or initiative, to raise awareness and provide the relevant tools and resources for the businesses to be able to demonstrate improvement. This is *conscious competence.*

'Right, pull over and switch the engine off!' Still on lesson three, and still grating the gears. Louise had had enough. 'Close your eyes. Put down the clutch. Start in first, that's right. Second, over to third, then fourth. Now again.' After five minutes of 'blind gear changes,' I'd got it. Success every time provided I thought about it. I'd become consciously competent.

Conscious competence requires effort

The last box is where you are aiming for as an organization. Your staff instinctively shares knowledge; and learning before, during and after any event is the norm. They don't pick up the telephone and ask a consultant for advice – managing knowledge has become second nature. This is *unconscious competence.* At this stage the knowledge is tacit. You have to be questioned to consider how you do it. BP hasn't arrived here yet, certainly not across all of its business units – it remains our aspiration.

After lesson five, I made it – unconsciously competent. Painless gear changes just 'happened,' and I selected the right gear instinctively. I had become an expert!

… but unconscious competence is the goal

This four-step model can be used to describe the stages for embedding knowledge management in BP.

We started by listening to what was already going on inside the organization, and identifying successful examples. For example, the drilling team in the Gulf of Mexico who had built an unprecedented three days for reflection and learning into their project plans, and saved millions of dollars with every well that they drilled as a result. Stories like these were told around the company as implicit challenges to the way other businesses operated – awakening them to their unconscious incompetence.

As we learned more of what was going on inside and outside the company, we began to create some models to describe knowledge management, and tried to focus the diverse set of tools and processes into a few key ones – tools for learning before, during and after an event. These tools helped to raise the level of competence in different parts of the company, from Japan to Alaska, as members of a small central team of internal consultants worked with business teams to transfer the skills and thereby demonstrate the real-world relevance of this particular management buzzword.

One team member worked on a project to construct self-service retail sites in Japan, something that had never been done before in that part of the world. Another member worked with refinery operators to improve their ability to shut down and recommission the plant in record time.

Success breeds success These projects in turn generated their own success stories, and began to spread the word at a grass-roots level, that knowledge management was relevant, and that these tools and techniques had real, bottom-line impact. A series of fires had been lit across the company. These fires were brought together in a community of practice – the 'knowledge management community'.

Make it part of the way you work The final phase – the one which BP is still working in – is what happens after the initiative phase is over, when the message has been heard by most, understood by many and applied by some. Shortly after the BP-Amoco merger, the central, knowledge-management function was disbanded, and the emphasis placed on embedding the all-important KM principles into the company's core processes. Growing closer to unconscious competence, the organization is putting knowledge management practices into its everyday business activity, and embedding the lessons.

We couldn't find any way of moving directly from unconscious incompetence to unconscious competence – we found that implementation of any programme requires time to be spent in all four steps. We are working hard to reduce the time to competency. The approach we took is summarized in the five points below:

- Look for what's already going on inside the company. Find some heroes.

- Check the external world for good practices and test them inside the organization.

- Focus on a few key tools and promote them. Make it simple and avoid creating a new language.

- Work in depth in a few critical areas to prove the value.

- Look to the existing company processes and 'infect them' with KM principles.

So, knowledge management is about connecting to those who know the recipe more than capturing an encyclopaedia of knowledge. Knowledge itself can be held in people's heads and it can be written down. Both sources should be used. It's about striking the right balance of people, process and technology. Knowledge is not just captured or shared, it is also created, discovered, distilled, validated, transferred, adopted, adapted and applied. Knowledge is richer than data and information; it's about familiarity gained from experience.

It's difficult to manage knowledge, but you can create and nurture the environment for knowledge sharing to flourish. The aim is for knowledge management to become an unconscious competence.

The Holistic Model
– It's More Than
the Sum of the Parts

So now we know what knowledge management is and isn't, what can we do? In this chapter we discuss:

• Using a model to provide a framework.

• Turning business objectives into business results.

• Learning before, during and after.

• Accessing and applying the know-how of the community.

• Making use of all parts of the model.

• Applying the model consistently.

It was 11.30 p.m. on a dark autumn night. John and Rachel were just returning home from a night out at the theatre. On turning a sharp bend in the road, they saw car headlights shining upwards at a crazy angle somewhere just off the road to the right of them. Then they noticed a fresh gap in the wooden fence. John stopped the car, put on his hazard flashers, and rushed through the gap in the fence and across a ploughed field, with Rachel in pursuit.

A hundred metres into the field was a car with a single occupant half out of the car. John quickly took charge and despatched Rachel back to the car to drive to the nearest village to phone for an ambulance. He told her to get the first-aid kit and a torch from the rear of their Mercedes.

John noticed the badly distorted leg of the driver, hanging awkwardly from the car. He cursed Rachel for having driven off before coming back with the first-aid kit and torch. With a brief shiver he removed his own shirt, quickly put his jacket back on, and tore the shirt into strips to make a bandage. Clearly this was no time to wait or worry about what Rachel would say about his shirt. He struggled to recall what his first-aid training had been, some 15 years previously, then pulled the leg straight before tying two ankles together, to keep the tension on the broken leg. He then applied a further bandage to stem the flow of bleeding.

It was then he smelled the leaking fuel, and decided to drag the occupant from the car to a safer spot, away from the risk of fire. He struggled to undo the safety belt in the distorted cabin, but then dragged the casualty away across the muddy field. By the time he had moved 25 metres from the car he was feeling exhausted and slumped down by the casualty.

He saw the blue flashing light before he heard the siren. His wife was still not back. He rushed to meet the accident crew, flushed with pride that he had immobilized the leg.

The accident crew checked for pulse and circulation. There was none – the driver had died in the crash.

What has this to do with knowledge management? If John had a model in mind he would have checked the casualties overall health. The Red Cross teaches the ABC model – Airways, Breathing, Circulation – as the first checks on a casualty.

Why are models helpful?

Knowledge management is a complex area, and one which spans boundaries – learning and development, information technology, human resources. Having a model that describes the scope of activity that your knowledge management efforts cover, can be a powerful way to both monitor and communicate what your approach encompasses.

As a team, we spent several meetings and many, many discarded flipcharts before arriving at the model shown below. Our model relates learning processes, and the capture and transfer of knowledge to day-to-day business. Once we had a common view, it enabled us to identify any gaps or shortcomings in our approach, and to take steps to address them.

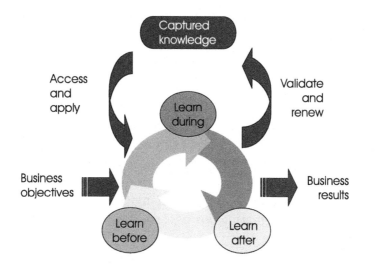

Whilst any step in isolation will make some difference, the real benefit will come from applying knowledge management holistically. This ensures that the end result is greater than the sum of its parts, and that the learning process is

The power of a common view

sustained. In the last chapter we described how the *framework* includes discovering, capturing, adapting, adopting, distilling, validating, sharing, and applying knowledge. It embraces people, process, and technology with equal importance. In order to excel at sharing what we know, and to capture meaningful knowledge, we require a common framework and the right set of skills.

One powerful example that so impressed BP that they used it as part of their corporate advertising campaign, was the approach to the Development Drilling programme on Schiehallion oil field, north of Scotland.

> *'The capture and transfer of know-how from the Foinaven (north of Scotland) and Gulf of Mexico assets was a major factor in reducing the planned development costs by $50 million.'*
>
> Development manager

Reusing knowledge is faster than recreating it. We have seen from people's experience that teams can 'have the time to halve the time', and use this increased productivity to create the space to share and learn more. By concentrating on what you need to *know*, then finding out the best way to learn it before focusing on what we need to *do*, the outcome is achieved faster and with less effort.

At the highest level, most companies work by setting business objectives for their staff, who in turn use knowledge to deliver business results. The first question we asked was:

'How can knowledge management make a difference in this simple process of getting business results from business objectives?'

We believed that the key to this was to introduce learning at every opportunity. The first part of the holistic model is to ensure we learn *before*, *during* and *after* everything we do.

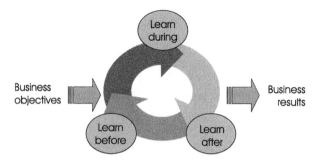

- *Learning before*. If you are about to start a task, it is likely that someone, inside or outside the company has done something similar before. *Why are we doing this? Are we sure we are setting off on the right activity? What can be learned from them? If we can reuse some knowledge, will this save us time to concentrate on activities that have not been undertaken before?*

- *Learning during*. Is what we have been doing likely to achieve our desired outcome? What can we learn about *what* we have been doing and *how* we are doing it? Is what is happening what we intended? We do this when we want to continuously improve based on reviewing our actions to date. It is easy to become blinkered whilst in the middle of a project – everybody needs to 'come up for air' at times and reflect on what has already been achieved.

Learning before, during and after

- *Learning after*. Most of our activities are not one-time events. When we do something again, *how* can we do it better than the last time, and *how* can we capture and share what we have learned? Who could make use of what you have learned? As an organization we reviewed significant joint ventures and mergers with other companies to develop the capability for doing it again even more effectively.

Another key element of the holistic model is shown below.

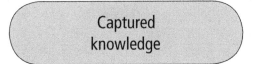

This means capturing the know-how in such a way that it can be reused. Knowledge needs storing for reuse; you cannot just leave it in people's heads. If you can find an effective way to capture it for transfer, others can look for it and find it, and the know-how will stay in the corporation even if the staff leave. One of the best ways to store know-how for effective reuse is by building a knowledge asset.

There needs to be a link between the learning before/during/ after circle and the knowledge itself, both to accessing what has already been captured and to capturing new knowledge. Networks and communities of practice are the primary route for enabling this access. We likened this to the way customers use a bank – making a withdrawal from a 'knowledge bank' at the start of a project and depositing new knowledge at the end.

Let's look at the elements in a little more detail.

Learn before doing

Typically we would learn before starting any new piece of work. Examples include: entering a new market, assessing commercial options or, troubleshooting a manufacturing problem.

- It's likely someone has done this before. Make it the norm for any activity to find out what knowledge *is out there* before performing any piece of work.

- Try a search of your intranet or the Internet, using a search engine, or corporate yellow pages (see Chapter 10, Finding the Right People) to find out where the experience lies in your company.

  In one example, a manager from BP Chemicals in SE Asia searched for information on a particular fuel's additive; within five minutes he had found something on the company intranet in the US that was worth £10,000 to his business. As search technologies are steadily improving, becoming smarter, more precise and more proactive, examples like these should be on the increase.

- Put together a peer assist meeting, so people with the knowledge can come and help with your problem (see Chapter 7 for more on peer assists).

Learn during the activity

Routinely performed, 'learning during' activity will be of real benefit to team delivery.

- Learn from yourselves! Introduce simple techniques such as the After Action Review (AAR), a short team meeting to capture operational knowledge as you go (see Chapter 8 for more on AARs). BP in Vietnam introduced AARs to learn how to negotiate with the Vietnamese, and ended up rethinking their negotiating strategy as a result.

- Learn from others. There are probably others out there facing similar problems to you on a day-to-day basis. Set up a community of practice – perhaps little more than a distribution list of interested parties – so you can tap into their know-how when you need it.

Learning after doing

Learn
after

A process of 'learning after doing' is valuable for the team, and helps them perform the next job better. It is also valuable for others who may face the same challenges you have just faced, either immediately, or at some time in the future.

- Stop and hold a meeting so the team can reflect on what has happened. Even if you do not write anything down, you will carry the knowledge with you to the next project. However, writing it down is better. Putting knowledge into a searchable store is better still, since human memories fade unless backed up by something recorded.

- Hold a retrospect or some form of post-project appraisal in order to draw lessons and insights from those involved.

OK. So that tells you a bit about learning before, during and after everything we do. So where do we get it from, where do we store it?

Captured
knowledge

Think of the difference between a magazine article and a textbook. The magazine tells you just enough to get you interested, you can read an article in ten minutes, all in one go. The article also gives references of where to go if you want to find out more.

Captured knowledge requires some context and also a collection of specific experiences that are 'distilled' to provide the content. BP labels called such a collection a 'knowledge asset'. We found that this approach retains context as well as content, and provides the back-up material that someone may need in the future. Capture the knowledge in a simple but engaging way. We have learned that you do not have to write down everything you do, but capture the highlights and tell the story.

Like a magazine article

It is vital to ask *who* knows, as well as *what* does the organization know. In the earlier example of the Schiehallion oil field (see p. 34), it was the drilling network that transferred the learning rapidly so the new team did not start at the bottom of the learning curve.

Even though we can capture knowledge, we cannot possibly capture everything. A lot of operational knowledge and experience will always remain in the heads of the practitioners, as tacit knowledge that we cannot codify easily. To make the best use of what BP knows, we build relationships with others who want to learn, and from whom we can learn. We call these sorts of knowledge-sharing groups 'networks' and 'communities'. They are the keys mechanisms for exchanging knowledge in BP. Some networks are formal and have clear objectives, while others are less formal (see Chapter 11 for more details).

The final stage it to embed this captured knowledge into business processes. Knowledge is created from business activity, and needs to be embedded back into activity if it is to make a sustainable improvement to the business. In order to do this, the knowledge passes through a life cycle of a number of steps:

Embed captured knowledge back into the business process

- *Identify*, through some process of reflection, and pass into 'team history'.

- Analyse and *capture*, and draw out the lessons learned, record and package.

- After capturing enough experience, *validate* and distil the lessons into an approved set of guidelines – a knowledge asset.

- *Embed* these guidelines into the business process, so that they reach the people who need to use them.

- *Apply* and use them in business activity.

Reinforce the culture of learning and sharing Capturing know-how is not sufficient on it's own. It is far better if people already have a desire to give and to receive knowledge. Somehow you have to nurture the right behaviours and foster a supportive company culture. An example of supportive culture is one that recognizes and rewards employees and teams for sharing and using learning in their day-to-day activities.

A 'chicken and egg' factor works to reinforce this:

Learning tools and techniques can help create a favourable culture and sharing behaviours, and these behaviours and culture will be receptive to learning tools.

Introduction of learning tools

Knowledge-sharing behaviours

Success stories

Demand for new tools

Supportive culture

The trick is to start somewhere, and the virtuous circle will begin. Encouraged and inspired by success stories, every employee in the organization should be able to make some contribution to reinforcing this culture:

> 'In order to generate extraordinary value for shareholders, a company has to learn better than its competitors and apply that knowledge throughout its businesses faster and more widely than they do. The way we see it, anyone in the organization who is not directly accountable for making a profit should be involved in creating and distributing knowledge that the company can use to make a profit.'
>
> Sir John Browne, Harvard Business Review, 1997

So having established a model, how do you use it?

The entry point can be almost anywhere. It's possible to start with various elements of this model and extend to embrace the whole model. If you have just taken stock of where you are with your current project and want to know what next, use the holistic model as a template. Perhaps you should take what you've learned and build on a new or existing knowledge asset, or perhaps it prompts a request you can make of the network.

Finding the right place to start – anywhere!

In BP's Vietnam operations, the first step was to introduce AARs to enable the business to review their progress with negotiations. Negotiations with host governments are often lengthy, complex and necessary before the company is prepared to make a large financial investment. The business was keen to try another tool. By using the model as a framework and marking the areas that were addressed, the learning before, during and after components could be 'ticked off' in turn.

Using the model as a checklist for KM activity

The model prompted the business leadership to consider who the community of practice (see Chapter 11) was for their particular activity. Ten separate negotiations were ongoing but only four people in the business unit had an overview of all ten. Some issues were commercially sensitive so it made sense limiting that knowledge to a few – but more *could* be shared. The best exchange seemed to occur when everyone sat down for lunch together in the Hanoi office, hence the immediate community became all those involved in the ten negotiations, the management team and representatives from the local Vietnamese staff.

The business set up a 'war room' in Hanoi, a project room, a physical knowledge store in one of the offices. On the walls of a dedicated room, they pinned up charts made of the deal process, and of the structure of the Vietnam government organization ... the 'stakeholder analysis'. People met in the room to prepare for meetings and to review the meetings. They had listed the key issues on the wall and they could discuss who they were seeing and the next steps in the negotiation. They could also discuss the interaction between different threads of the negotiation.

The Vietnam business captured a summary of the key AARs each week and reviewed them at the weekly management meeting. The management team used this in considering the priorities for the next negotiations.

How do we make this model add up to more than the sum of the parts?

We can see a result once people are using the tools of learning before, during and after, and are interacting with the store of knowledge, and the knowledge is being used and refreshed. The community of people interested in that knowledge feel responsible for keeping it current, they find it useful, and so they tap into it and learn before doing. They capture what they have learned and add it to the knowledge asset. They tidy up the store – remove unwanted or out-of-date knowledge and distil it so it is easy to reach the parts that make a difference. This generates a system which is reinforcing and self-sustaining.

Applying the model consistently

One of the biggest challenges we have faced
is to stop people doing things differently each
time. The nature of BP's operations has resulted
in a strong engineering culture in which staff
thrive on space to innovate – learning before is still a key step
to innovating.

Reinforcing and
sustaining

In the last chapter we explored the route to unconscious competence. At the earlier stage of conscious competence it is key
to adopt a consistent approach in order to make it routine.
Persisting with a model even when it doesn't work first time, or
every time, is important.

For a golfer it's a bit like teaching your muscles how to swing
the club properly. The pro gives you a set of points to think
about before each swing of the club. At first you are thinking so
hard about facing the club to the ball, getting your feet right,
keeping your head down, taking the club back slowly that you
miss the ball completely. Only once the pro distracts you does
your unconscious take over and you hit the ball cleanly. It takes
many months (did I hear you utter 'years'?) of practice for your
muscles to learn the unnatural swing, so that it becomes an
unconscious competence.

The idea of offering a model is to provide a consistent approach
to managing knowledge so that a practitioner can repeat the
approach several times until the muscles are trained to do it
naturally. At that stage the model can be dispensed with and the
practitioner unconsciously applies the techniques.

So, whilst learning to be competent, choose an approach and
persistently stick to it. Once you are consciously competent
then you can allow your unconscious to take over. At that stage
being clear on your desired outcome (knowing which way the
green is, and how far it is), and ensuring actions are consistent
with getting you there (selecting the appropriate club, bearing
in mind where the bunkers are and how well you are playing

today) is probably more appropriate than always following the same approach.

> *'When we define where we want to be, all of our actions turn out to be congruent with that place.'*
>
> Phil Forth, consultant

Over the course of our implementation of knowledge management, we have developed this simple holistic model to use as a framework. At the end of the day, it is *only a model!*

We invite you to try it out in your own working environment. If the model serves to align and focus your actions, then it has value. If it leads to the creation of a different model then that is even better, and the authors would love to hear from you.

The real business benefits come from working on all parts of the model and embedding the activities into the routine business processes. This develops a sustainable capability rather than an ongoing dependency on 'experts'.

We've discussed what knowledge management is and proposed a model for framing it, but how do we create the right environment for knowledge to flow?

In this chapter we discuss:

- Removing the barriers for information sharing.

- A common operating environment.

- Peer processes.

- The right behaviours.

- Leadership.

- Community approach.

- Managing change.

- Recognizing existing strengths.

We are wondering how many of you have experienced the same embarrassment? The embarrassment of the school

The embarrassment of
the school dance

dance. There we are in the school hall, which is camouflaged with bright decorations and balloons. The lights are dimmed. The boys are at one end, close to where the soft drinks and refreshments are served. The girls, from the same co-educational school or the local high school, cluster at the other end near to the aspiring band from the school.

When the band takes a break and recognizable rhythms emanate from the DJ's turntable many of the girls start dancing with each other. Eventually, usually only 30 minutes before the end of the evening, the bolder boys, perhaps encouraged by illicit refreshments, move in to claim a dance with their favourite girl of the evening. In some cases the girls do not wait and drag their dream man onto the floor.

The last slow dance fills the floor with hugging couples, whilst those around the periphery dream of what might have been. All too soon the harsh lights of the hall switch on, revealing the acne, and dampening the ardour of all but the most passionate of couples. And the environment is exposed for what it really is - the school hall.

For a few precious hours the organizing committee have done a great job of converting the hall into an environment for romance to flourish.

So how do we create an attractive, sustainable environment for the sharing of know-how? What are the barriers to be removed?

Understanding the barriers to sharing

Firstly there is the barrier of technology. I struggle to share a document electronically with you because you are not connected to my network. It could be because you don't use the same software as me or you have a more recent version of the software that does not recognize my version. Maybe I have mistyped your e-mail address. So I send you a CD with the document on. Perhaps I have compressed it to make sure I can get the figures included and you don't have the decompression software. Does any of this sound familiar to you?

Then there is the barrier of the business processes and the way we organize ourselves. Even within the same office we struggle to share something that would be useful to another department because we focus totally on the tasks the department have to complete by that fast-approaching deadline. Sometimes our goals put us in direct competition with other parts of the organization.

How often have you been to a meeting when you have prepared your position beforehand? You feel good about the meeting because you have prepared well. Unfortunately someone you work alongside chooses to take a counter position and she has done her preparation well also. The general manager who is chairing the meeting allows you each to keep debating your positions in an attempt to win over 'the other side'. The meeting overruns, no agreement is reached, and tempers are frayed. The only action agreed is to meet again in a week's time to discuss the topic further.

I wonder if the people in the meeting above were actively listening to each other's argument to check that they understood it. Did they take the time to acknowledge the point, or were they merely using the time the other was speaking to construct the next point of argument?

Finally there is the barrier of people's behaviour. In BP, with many trained engineers and other graduates, the culture was one of not showing signs of weakness by having to ask for help. If someone did ask for help, you were too busy anyway with your own priorities, and your boss would not approve of you helping another department.

We can tackle each of these barriers separately, but by addressing the three together we will ensure the creation of an attractive environment for knowledge sharing.

Connecting the company via a common operating environment

BP is on the third version of a 'common operating environment' (COE), a standard for computers, software and communications. This has been implemented across the former BP, Amoco, Arco and Burmah-Castrol companies, reaching some 110,000 people. The cost of doing this was significant ($300 million). What are the benefits to a company like BP?

Everyone is connected. They can share documents and information across the globe quickly by having the same standard software, hardware and naming conventions. They can dock into, and log onto, the company network and access their e-mail, their personal and shared documents from any BP office in the world, from Alaska to Vietnam, from China to Mexico. In addition they can connect from home, from the airport or from the hotel room. They can stay connected from wherever they are in the world.

They can quickly share documents, store them in a common place, use common search and access methods, and have discussion forums to tap into the diversity of expertise within the organization. They can jointly collaborate on the construction of a presentation or document without physically being in the same place. Although none of these capabilities are truly 'leading edge', the ability to be able to work in this way across an entire organization, every day, is extremely powerful. It removes so many of the barriers to sharing.

Common is more important than current

In order to do this they have to give up some independence. They have similar hardware, the same software and the same version of that software. They do not always move to the latest version. For instance, BP used Windows 95 as the operating system for five years after it was first released! *Common* is more important than *current*. There was a time when one of the business streams had standardized on Apple Macintosh computers. They swapped them for IBM Windows PCs, in the interests of sharing with the whole organization.

> The common operating environment has been a great enabler, but on its own is not sufficient to ensure the sharing of know-how. Think about your own organization. What are the barriers in your organization to sharing knowledge?

Processes

BP uses a number of peer processes to improve the sharing of knowledge company-wide.

Develop peer processes

The effective management of know-how and knowledge is central to both the delivery of today's performance and to the future success of the company. The key to real success in being a knowledge-based company is in the way they organize themselves, and the behaviours they exhibit. Experience has shown that an organization based on a federation of self-standing business units is very good for delivering financial performance, but is not ideal for transferring know-how around the company. For this reason they have created a number of so-called peer processes:

- peer groups share know-how amongst senior group managers at the portfolio and resource allocation level;

- peer reviews expose specific business activities to the challenge and scrutiny of senior professionals and leaders from similar business activities around the group; and

- peer assists are used at the professional specialist level to make sure the right know-how gets to the right place at the right time.

They also encourage all staff to become members of lateral networks across the organization – where they belong to communities with similar interests. They believe outstanding business performance comes from liberating staff, creating a culture where they feel comfortable asking for and offering help.

So BP has put peer processes in place to improve the sharing of know-how between businesses. Not every process encourages sharing of know-how however. One group of businesses were set a target of reducing running costs by 25 per cent with a clear implication that those under-performing would be sold. The businesses had survival on their mind rather than sharing, especially with 'competitors' within the same organization. Common goals engender a spirit of win-win, that is, everyone can succeed whilst helping others by sharing what they know.

Back to that meeting that you prepared so well for earlier. A more successful meeting can deliver results by encouraging an atmosphere of sharing experiences and then working together on creating a solution. For more on this process see Chapter 7 – 'Learning from your Peers', p. 97.

> Whether you belong to a large or small organization, have you considered using some peers – inside or outside – to help design your piece of work? How was your work improved as a result?

Behaviours

Make it easy to ask for help

'Help' is a four-letter word! It's a word we all know the meaning of, but are reluctant to utter. We have been educated to solve problems ourselves. If we have not done something before then we are encouraged to figure out how to achieve it. We often consider it a sign of weakness to ask someone else for some help. It's amazing how willing people are to give up their time if someone asks for help. The requestor gets lots of support to do a better job than he could have done on his own. At the very least he considers a wider range of opportunities.

One colleague of ours, Frank, used this facet of human behaviour when he wanted to share something he felt was a good practice. He was frustrated that his good ideas had been ignored before. This time he had a great process for prioritizing IT services.

Instead of making a presentation to 'sell' his idea, he requested help to improve his process. The result? He improved his process still further and three people took his process away to implement at their own offices.

> Why not get together with some colleagues and brainstorm answers to the questions 'how can we make it easy to ask for help' and 'how can we make it easy to offer help in our organization?'

To encourage people to offer their help we advocate rewarding people who exhibit the right behaviours. Peer recognition is the most powerful motivation we have experienced, receiving acknowledgement that their contribution made a difference. Within BP some businesses include a review of sharing know-how as an integral part of their annual appraisal.

We share things better with people we know and trust. Would you lend your watch to a total stranger? Now would you lend your watch to your neighbour at work? It's the same with knowledge. Phil Forth, a consultant who routinely works with us, put it this way:

Sharing with someone you know

> *'I wouldn't share a secret with a roomful of people'.*

Instead he shares something minor to see if there is the basis for a relationship and then looks for reciprocity and trust to develop.

We are going to need to develop new ways of forming relationships, as we routinely get knowledge from others via the Web, or across a large organization, without meeting face-to-face. We have not solved that yet, and when time and money permit we meet face-to-face as a precursor to exchanging know-how. Indeed, a key part of the process between the authors and the publishers of this book was to meet and lunch together in order to develop rapport. Many of the subsequent exchanges have been held via phone or e-mail. In the world of e-business we may not be able to meet all of our customers face-to-face. We will have to find new ways to develop rapport electronically.

'"Connectedness and openness" have taken over from "secrecy and empire building" as keys to personal and collective success.'

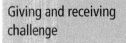
Active listening Whether with a friend or a stranger, sharing of knowledge is better if people develop active listening skills. What is active listening? Our definition is that you spend time understanding what a person means, and replaying it in your own words to check that understanding as a precursor to stating if you agree with it and why. 'So you mean to say that if I say what I heard back to you, then we'll both have a clearer understanding?' That's right! In our experience, too may people queue up to speak rather than listen to what others have to say.

Giving and receiving challenge Another behaviour that is key to sharing knowledge is giving and receiving a challenge. Challenging assumptions or someone's firmly held beliefs takes some effort, as does receiving such a challenge.

> In the course of reading this book, you have probably read something that you wish to challenge us on, haven't you? Have a think about how you might do it in a way that would not cause offence or defence.

Leadership

In our experience, great leadership is demonstrated by people who exhibit good active listening, who check their understanding, who ask 'What have you learned from others?' and who acknowledge when they have learned something from you. No one likes to be told to change their behaviour by someone clearly not exhibiting that behaviour ('Do as I say, not as I do ... ').

When Centrica's senior directors met to discuss how to improve knowledge sharing in the company, they came up with a list of challenging questions for everyone in a leadership position:

- How can I personally demonstrate that 'asking for help' is a sign of strength rather than weakness?

- When encountering a business problem, how can I reinforce the importance of learning from others – rather than simply providing an answer?

- When reviewing a project or investment proposal, have I ensured that it brings to bear knowledge from other projects?

- How do I react when someone fails – is it viewed purely as a loss to the business, or as a need for investment in their education?

> Why not develop your own list of the ideal 'leadership behaviours' which would make a difference in your organization?

Like most large organizations, Centrica has a regular annual intake of university graduates and postgraduates, recruited as potential future senior leaders for the company. Around 50 join in the UK each October, participating in **Build knowledge-sharing into management development** specialist or general management development programmes with at least four job rotations during the first two years including a mandatory operational, customer-facing role. During this time they each benefit from a 'buddy relationship' with a graduate from a previous year's intake. The graduates meet as a group regularly during these early years, coming together for induction and development programmes, training courses and learning set meetings, supported by their own intranet portal, dedicated newsletter and a hectic year-round calendar of self-organized social events.

With strategic understanding, shared experiences, regular meetings, strong relationships and an intense desire to learn and succeed, the graduates have all the ingredients of an effective support network. Sam, a graduate from 2003, who is buddied with James from the 'class of 2002', picks up the story:

> 'With James working within marketing at the AA Insurance, and my role working in customer services within British Gas, there did not seem too many opportunities to knowledge share and exchange our experiences. However, after about three months in the business I changed roles and after numerous conversations with James we struck gold. My role in customer retention revolves around the involvement of front line staff in identifying ways to retain our customers.
>
> James' role within the AA looks at a similar problem but from a marketing perspective with very little involvement of the front line staff. This provided the opportunity for James to have a look at the retention activity within British Gas to see what could successfully translate to the AA.'

Recognizing this powerful opportunity to network operational issues around the company, in 2004, the role of the Centrica graduate was enlarged. In addition to delivering in their own department, and developing and learning as professionals, each of them now has a responsibility to identify good practices and actively share with their peers – and to help other staff to tap into their connections too. Their intranet portal now carries a register of good practices that have been transferred, and their newsletter has a regular feature on knowledge sharing success stories.

Andrea Vowles, who manages the Graduate Programme concludes:

> '... as a manager in Centrica receiving a placement graduate, you now get much more than a young talented individual. You get access to an extended network of talented individuals who are committed to finding and sharing the best ideas and examples that they can find – from anywhere in the company.'

The long term benefit is that Centrica has an increasing talent pool rising up the company, who have already developed the good habits of asking for, and offering help to their colleagues.

> How does your organization nurture and develop future leaders? Are there ways in which you could influence this, and create a 'rising pool' of knowledge-sharers?

What have other organizations done to create the right environment? Let's look now at a primary school in Australia.

Community approach

Noumea is a public primary school in the state of New South Wales in Australia with some 580 students. It receives extra funding because it is officially classified as a disadvantaged school. It is situated in an area with high unemployment and high crime rates, housing is provided by the state and there are 50+ ethnic groups in the community. A high barbed wire fence surrounds the school. In its early years parents felt uncomfortable coming into the school many having experienced failure during their own education, others seeing school as an extension of government authority. These fears are still reflected in many families that enrol at the school each year. Literacy and numeracy were and continue to be an issue amongst parents as well as students. The school is viewed as a place to solve learning and social problems that continually arise in the community. Up to 40% of students leave and enrol each year and 80% of teachers are always in their first four years of teaching. The school was headed by six principals in the space of ten years. A high turnover of staff and students meant the school was suffering with performance and behaviour problems, with a culture of fear and failure, and with a lost sense of identity. More significantly it was suffering from a loss of institutional memory. Quite a challenge!

The starting point was to hold community meetings inviting parents, students, teachers, and administrative staff, with a view to encouraging the participation of all stakeholders. Offering food and drink ensured a good attendance – morning coffee, tea parties, barbeques etc. The incoming principal, Jenny Lewis, challenged the community to make a difference,

'We can either sink, or swim out of here with gold medals.'

Extra government funding enabled the school to offer literacy, numeracy, technology and health and nutrition programmes to parents enabling them to support their own children in the home. Because of the inevitable reluctance to admit illiteracy, it started with a small number, but the participants soon encouraged others along. The school provided baby-sitting services to enable more to attend. Serendipity played its part too, with other parents rooting for the newly formed junior rugby league team. It united parents across ethnic divides along the touchline, and raised the esteem of the school when they started winning!

As teachers got to know parents at these social events, a few parents volunteered to help in the running of the school. Today there are some 40-50 parents playing a role in the school each day. These parents naturally act as advocates for the school, sharing successes back in the community.

Learn from others An early activity was to learn how other schools were tackling similar challenges. Teams were established to investigate different issues especially what was working in the UK and US inner city schools. Parents and teachers together contacted other schools around the world learning of their experiences.

By talking and sharing values as a community they came to understand that *disadvantaged* did not mean *dumb*; by learning about and appreciating each other's culture they realized that each has different knowledge and experiences to share. Some of the ethnic groups for example had a very matriarchal society, which was very different from others. School community members came to recognize that diversity provided the opportunity and the potential for everyone to be successful.

This building of common values was not a one-time event. There are 250 new people coming into the school each year. It starts with an

Develop shared values

interview of the family, usually conducted by the clerical staff rather than the principal. They are not figures of authority; they are part of the community and can have a better discussion.

When Jenny Lewis arrived at the school the structures in place were conventional, middle class and 'looking how they looked 50 to 60 years ago.' Six principals in ten years had introduced a number of procedures to fix things. Processes had been added and nothing taken away. So the community set about challenging these legacy systems, asking *why* and *for what purpose?*

Situated in the staff room was a *'What-cheeses-me-off'* board where people could share their frustrations, have a laugh and usually someone

Challenge convention

would offer a practical solution. Conventional assumptions were challenged, for example, the timing of breaks and lunch. Some students arrived at school hungry, not having eaten that day. Energy levels and concentration were low. The school introduced an early break with food and drink and quality time to run around. That prepared them for a good work session in the morning. Another practical solution came by acknowledging that students progressed at different rates – so instead of moving through the grades by year group, students moved according to their learning progress. Typically there is a three to four year age range in any class. Some accelerate and move quickly through the school, others can 'book in' to get an extra year to prepare them for high school. It is an option for parents and students to take advantage of, if they choose.

Openness and sharing are values the community hold dear and the principal sets the example. Every teacher knows what the principal knows.

Be a role model for openness and sharing

Electronic and paper mail is copied on immediately. There are three whiteboards side by side in the school - what's coming up this year, this month and this week. No one is surprised by upcoming events. Communities of practice have been developed both virtually and physically within the school encouraging staff to create and share new learnings.

Information from nine drawers around the school has been put together in one place. School staff developed a computer system called *Schoolmate* that allows a teacher to look at the story of the whole child. It contains the normal things such as monitoring of curriculum progress, test results, but what makes it special is that it is a reflective process. Teachers can record their reflections on a student or class and can reinforce what is being taught in other subjects. It makes it easy to identify inconsistent judgements of a student by different teachers. Students can record their own notes and access part of the system. As well as academic progress, social issues such as time away from school and behaviour are tracked and linked. For example, one child's misbehaviour was tracked to the days her mother attended a drug rehabilitation clinic.

Initially this system did place additional demands on teachers' time, but because they had designed it they were determined to make it successful, and they modified it until it worked for them. Today a teacher typically logs on for only three to five minutes a day. This system is improving the efficiency of learning at the school - *the focus being on learning work rather than busy work.*

Noumea has made good progress and they learned some powerful lessons on their way to creating a learning environment:

1   Gain the participation of all the stakeholders - and get them acquainted socially.

2   Challenge conventional structures and processes - push for more flexibility to achieve the desired outcomes.

3   Recognize the benefits of sharing knowledge – identify what is the key knowledge to share.

4   Make use of technology as an enabler – by knowing what it is capable of and then developing the capacity to use it.

> *'Noumea now looks like, feels like and smells like a learning community.'*

This is a remarkable turnaround of a school's performance. However you can't always get it right first time, but if you take the view that there is no failure only feedback, then next time around you'll do it better as this next story shows.

Managing change

Ken Brierley of British Nuclear Fuels plc (BNFL) observes:

> *'My experience with KM has evolved over the past six years from an interested observer, to a disciple, then a fully-fledged evangelist taking a full-time functional role in KM. In BNFL we developed a KM strategy and instituted several KM initiatives. These achieved success at a local level within the specific part of the business but we subsequently failed to gain enterprise-wide implementation. Eventually the local successes were eroded as new management came into the organization and failed to see the benefits.'*

Ken has now moved into a change management role, and spent time learning and understanding change management best practice with the help of some external experts in the field. It prompts him to shout from the rooftops:

> *'If only I knew then what I know now.*
> *'I realize now that we failed to gain enterprise-wide roll-out or even sustain localized improvement because we did not see our activity as change management. If I was starting over, the top five things I will do differently next time are:*

- *Executive buy-in is the major critical success factor - so plan to get it, make it visible, and work to maintain it.*
- *A stakeholder analysis together with a communications plan are essential for any major KM project and they require continuous review to check alignment with vision, scope and stakeholder issues.*

Deliver quick wins that are tangible, visible, symbolic and sustainable

- *Deliver "quick wins" which are tangible, highly visible, symbolic, and sustainable. They will provide evidence that KM can deliver the required improvements.*
- *A balanced set of measures, both leading and lagging, with targets will reinforce the vision and assure the required outcome.*
- *Planning for KM initiatives must include the transition from current-state to end-state, and the embedding of the change to become "operation as usual."'*

Like BNFL, Centrica have a simple methodology for the people-aspects of change management. Check out the CD resources for their checklist.

I believe those organizations successful with KM programmes either already have the key change management essentials in place and don't realize it, or take it for granted, or they may be mirroring our experience and heading for unsustainable KM performance when the next round of management changes and budget cuts occur.'

This resonates with me. I've been seconded into the UN to help create an environment for sharing knowledge to respond to the HIV/AIDS epidemic. In adapting some of the BP techniques to work in a different context, I'd taken for granted the essentials existing in BP during a change process that has been going on since 1989. Fortunately others in the field have been working hard to put these in place.

Facilitating the response to AIDS

For too long the response to HIV and AIDS has been driven by institutional interventions, such as the provision of basic education material. What if we reframed the issue and started with a belief that the capacity to respond is already there locally, and then found ways to support? Let's look at how a facilitative approach gives voice to *local* experience and knowledge. Here is a declaration from a group of 25 people from around the world who met in Zambia to share experience of facilitation as a way to reveal community strengths, to learn together and build human capacity to respond to HIV/AIDS.

'"We care for more than 200 orphans here in Kasisi," Sister tells our group, "Many of them are infants brought to us by families who have no choice: for those children it is either the orphanage or sure death, as there is no one in the family to breast feed the infant after the mother died. Many of those orphans return to their families once they are weaned. Forty-five children have AIDS; three of these get anti retroviral therapy (ART). I don't dare start ART for a fourth one. We are just unable to secure funding for the drugs; we have tried everywhere. A UN representative told us that the UN only works through government."

'We move from the orphanage to neighbouring communities to talk to families and visit Sarah, who is dying of AIDS. She has constant diarrhoea. Her mother and her sister stay next to her 24 hours a day, every day. Twelve other family members help in the background. The round, one-room house is clean, and the atmosphere is one of respect and love. Sarah's mother sits on the bed, frequently reaching out to her daughter as she speaks to us about the family's experience. Outside, Sarah's father and her sister, with a small child, stay close. The home-based care worker is groping for solutions. Pointing in all directions, he says, "There are so many people dying everywhere."

'Every community and family has some level of capacity to respond to HIV and AIDS and provide care for those affected - like Sarah and the

Recognize community strengths

45 children in the orphanage. Capacity can take the form of education programmes, distribution of condoms, and provision of care facilities. For communities to use their existing capacity and develop their potential further, facilitation is required. Facilitation creates opportunities for service providers and policy makers to learn together with communities and build on this capacity.

'During our visit, a member of the facilitation team involved in national policy was already seeking ways in which the sister might get ART, and how treatment might get to Sarah.'

The preconceptions of community weakness are challenged by seeing at first hand how communities and local organizations are responding in partnership to develop new ways of coping with orphans, or by recognizing the capacity of families to administer and monitor ART to ensure adherence. Through recognizing community strengths, organizations also recognize how working *with* rather than *for* people in communities will enhance the effectiveness of the services they provide. Through learning together, new solutions based on local experience can be developed. Experience shows that these solutions are the ones which last.

> Think who else you can involve in your activity to ensure that those affected can have a stake in the action and outcome.

We've looked at a variety of contexts, and some common threads emerge. Setting an enabling environment is fundamental to allowing sharing to happen naturally, and it has been achieved by:

1   A reinforcing leadership style, which challenges and encourages learning and sharing.

2   Encouraging the right behaviours; behaviours that acknowledge people's strengths, involve active listening, challenge the status quo, develop relationships and build trust.

3   Taking the time to understand each other, developing shared beliefs and a common vision.

4   Building facilitation skills to enable people to find their own solutions.

5   Good change management capabilities, for example include those affected in the planning, the execution and the outcome.

6   Collaborative working and learning together from shared experiences.

7   Common technology that connects people, removes barriers, and makes it information widely available.

So, having created the environment for knowledge to flow, now it's time to get started!

It's one thing understanding what knowledge management is. Understanding that the knowledge management model has several components, each of which adds value, is helpful. Getting the environment
right helps. But what then? We could spend a lifetime learning before
doing, but unless we get into action then we never achieve anything.

In this chapter:

- start with 'where the business is';

- stop procrastinating and just do something simple;

- review what you have done and set the next steps; and

- a knowledge store doesn't have to be electronic!

ow do *you* solve jigsaw puzzles? I usually sort out the
four corners and the edge pieces, put them together and
then work towards the middle. My sister collects similar
colours together. A friend starts with the first pieces he picks up
and compares them to the picture. His brother is more extreme,
as he puts it together without looking at the picture till he has
finished! Usually we each have a preferred strategy to get us
started, and we may modify our approach if we are struggling
to put it together.

Have you ever sat there and looked at the picture and the pieces until you have figured out how it all goes together? Unlikely. There are just too many parts to hold in your head at once. So it is with knowledge management. We want to learn before doing, but there comes a time when we just have to get started.

Start with where the business is

Understanding the critical business issues is not enough. Studying examples of what others have done is useful. The very next step is to do something, and learn from doing it. Very often when we discussed knowledge management with a business team they would say:

> '*We think this is really good. The only problem is that we don't have the time right now on top of everything else we have to do.*'

Our response to this was:

> '*What if we told you someone else has already done the very task you are about to do. We just need to find out who and what they learned.*'

Having the time to halve the time

We even invented a slogan 'Having the time to halve the time.' In other words if you make time to work on this it will save you a lot of time in the long run.

- In China, BP had entered into a new joint venture to build and operate a chemicals factory. What were the issues that they didn't know they needed to know?

- BP was developing a project in Vietnam to create a gas and power industry, in a country that has little money and a big need for power in order to develop. They had reached a stand-off in commercial negotiations.

'We were negotiating 10 independent commercial contracts. We needed assistance in managing information and relationships. Our first goal was to know if we could reach a deal.'

- In Europe, Bovis were building a large number of petrol filling stations for BP. Could they build them more efficiently?

- UNAIDS knew it was important to encourage horizontal sharing of successful responses to HIV/AIDS between communities. But how?

Do something simple

No amount of theory will actually impact your business results. It's time to stop procrastinating. Get up off your seat and start doing something! Ensure that what you do is simple – no need to create an air of mystique.

In China, the KM team found a simple question to ask, *'What do we need to learn?'* Then they listened to the responses. This was very much about learning before getting into action. This started a conversation with individuals and with small groups, speculating on the future by reflecting on the past.

> Start with a question or a review

What do *you* need to learn?

In Vietnam the question posed was *'What is your key issue?'* It was essentially a 'pause for breath', a review of what had, and had not, been achieved. What was interesting was the diversity of responses from the key people in the team. They each saw the issue from a different perspective.

In Europe, after the first petrol filling station had been completed, all those involved met to review the work. They followed the format of an After Action Review, borrowed from the US Army (see Chapter 8).

As a principle, if the business teams were already in action, the starting point was an After Action Review, starting with the four standard questions (see Chapter 8). The event under review might be a meeting, a successful negotiation or an unsuccessful advertising campaign. For example you may have been promoting a project to the board, failing to sell a new product to a customer, or attempting to secure funding for a new venture.

Review what you have done and set the next steps

In China the team listened carefully to all the questions. That night in the hotel room they summarized what they had heard and the differences between the responses. They designed some new questions based on the responses. 'What do you need to know next?'

In Vietnam, after three days of interviewing and refining the questions, the team felt that they had a good grasp of the key issues. They reviewed what they had learned with the management team, who were amazed by how much the questioning had revealed. It provoked further conversation between the management team, in which tacit knowledge flowed. For example, one of the key negotiators shared how he prepared for the forthcoming negotiation. His strong body language indicated that it was knowledge that he had obviously not thought to share with his peers before.

In Europe the team made changes to their processes and procedures and built the next station, faster and cheaper. They met again the next day to carry out the After Action Review, keen to improve further.

What then?

Let's look at how a practical, stepwise programme was implemented in Vietnam, as an example.

The role of the knowledge manager

The business appointed a knowledge manager to co-ordinate the whole process. Here's what he had to say:

> *'You need a dedicated resource. People don't do this stuff in their spare time. You need a central person, and also you need a person in each team who has bought into the process, otherwise it won't work. Choose someone who talks a lot! A KM person has to be a communicator, has to get out there, find information, and feed it back again. Establishing me as knowledge manager meant that I was the focal point for anyone. I could respond to gossip by offering knowledge in return; "Did you know this?" It became two-way.*
>
> *'We used AARs extensively. Each team had a 15 minute debrief using the AAR format, after each discussion with the government. This was a very powerful tool within the team. They could look back at what they did, and change what they were doing the next day.*
>
> *'The AAR proformas had a distribution list, and I produced a weekly consolidation and also lessons learnt, and put it out to everyone. The weekly summary was good; if people had no time to read the AARs I would summarize each one into two or three sentences and highlight the key stuff."*

See the CD for a description of the role of a knowledge manager.

> *'The meetings tended to be in Hanoi. People passed through the office on their way to and from the meeting. The "war room" had to be physical. The charts we made of the deal process, and of the structure of the Vietnam government organization were too big to go on a PC, so we had them on the wall with a pen at the side. People could contribute by*

using the pen; they did not have to log on. When we had a discussion we could go in the room, update the charts rapidly, share it easily.'

Bruce MacFarlane

For BP, the common operating environment has been a great enabler, but on its own it is not sufficient to ensure the sharing of know-how. in Vietnam, the team used a room for sharing. Think about your own organization. What is the best environment in your organization for sharing knowledge?

The key was keeping the system simple, concise and effective. Reviews took 15 minutes, weekly notes were one or two pages, the chart was simple, and the software was simple. Because the community of practice was entirely local, the knowledge was stored in a physical room and it encouraged interaction. The information was useful and accessible so people started going in there before the meetings too ...

Another thing we have learned is to determine our priorities. What do we need most to achieve the objectives of our organization? Collecting knowledge on everything will be an endless task. In Chapter 6 we introduce self-assessment as a means of determining gaps so that you can prioritize where to focus your knowledge management effort. The approach also highlights your strengths so it indicates what you might share with others. We have found it a good way to start the sharing conversation with others.

So, in summary:

- Don't procrastinate. Get started right away!

- Start with where the business is, review where they are compared to where they were meant to be and determine what you can learn from that.

- Do something simple.

- Review and plan the next steps.

- Determine your priorities.

The next seven chapters offer you some tools and techniques to help make that difference. If you like what you've heard so far, then you'll know what you are looking for. Consider what it will feel like when you have achieved what you are striving for.

- Identify what knowledge you have to share and learn using the self-assessment framework in Chapter 6.

- For learning before, look at Chapter 7.

- For learning whilst doing, go to Chapter 8, to give you time to reflect.

- Read Chapter 9, if you want to learn after doing.

- If you want to know *who* to talk to try Chapter 10, or Chapter 11 if it's developing a sense of community that you are looking for.

- Chapter 12 will give you some insights into capturing knowledge.

These are the building blocks of the holistic model.

Part II
Tools and Techniques

Connecting Sharers
with Learners –
Using Self-Assessment

Since writing the first edition of *Learning to Fly*, Geoff and Chris have moved to apply their knowledge beyond BP. Chris moved to Centrica, an international energy and essential services company based in the UK and Geoff was seconded to the UN AIDS Competence programme in Geneva for eighteen months (some people get all the luck!). During that time we have both reflected on the things we took for granted in BP's culture, and how we can impact the uptake of knowledge management in organizations. We arrived at the same conclusion, that self-assessment helps groups identify their strengths and their weaknesses, what knowledge they have to share and what to learn. It provides the compelling reason to invest in knowledge management. That's why we have drawn out our experiences into this new chapter.

In this chapter, we cover:

- The need for a common language in order to share.

- Building a self-assessment framework.

- Build, test and freeze.

- Using the self-assessment framework to create a dialogue.

- Knowledge-based benchmarking.

- The river diagram and stairs diagram – visualizing the results.

- A strategic planning tool.

- A vehicle for knowledge exchange.

- Identifying the knowledge to share and whom to share it with.

- Applying the approach to customer management, and the response to AIDS.

The girl in the turquoise bikini

At the age of fourteen, I had my first and only real-life *Baywatch* experience. It happened whilst I was on holiday with my parents in the South of France, near St Tropez. It was a scorching day, and I was cooling off in a welcoming Mediterranean, stirred by the wind. I was swimming about 50m out from the shore, when I heard someone shouting. It didn't sound like French - some Scandinavian language perhaps? I turned my head to see the swimmer who had called out - a blonde girl in what looked like it might be a turquoise bikini. My adolescent girl-radar registered her as a well-developed fifteen, so I smiled back, and subtly changed direction, wondering whether she was Swedish.

She shouted again, this time it sounded urgent, and this time I *did* recognize one word that she was repeating from my schoolboy French– *'m'aidé!'*, so I swam strongly towards her, reaching her as she dipped beneath the waves for the third time. I helped her to stay afloat and we shouted together *'m'aidé!'*, *'m'aidé!'*, whilst I waved both arms towards the shore. Between her shouts she was babbling frantically in another language, but somehow *'Parlez-vous Anglais?'* didn't seem appropriately comforting, so I stuck to shouting *'m'aidé!'*.

Within a minute or two we'd been spotted, and the coastguard was upon us in his rescue boat. The rest of the experience seemed to go into fast-forward, and in an instant I was back on the beach, glowing with pride but slightly dazed. The girl in the turquoise bikini was been taken to the nearby medic for a check-up. Her parents came over later that afternoon to thank me – it turned out that the family was from Finland.

I never did get her number.

The need for a common language in order to share

One of the most common excuses given by people for not receiving help or good practice from another part of an organization is 'Oh but you don't understand – our business is different. We do things differently here ...' or 'That might work in marketing, but here we need some ....'. 'That might work in the private sector but here ...' Sometimes it can sound like they don't *want* to be understood! Does any of this sound familiar to you?

Benchmarking is a popular way for an organization to identify performance gaps relative to 'external good practices', and has been the favourite tool of management consultants for many years. Usually, the benchmarking process involves some sort of assessment process, with participants being measured against a range of descriptions or performance indicators. The consultant then collects what works in the best performing organizations to share with others. The consultant becomes more knowledgeable but does the good practice get applied?

Applying benchmarking *within* or between cooperating organizations has a powerful, and beneficial, side effect for anyone working to stimulate knowledge sharing – it creates a common language. It provides a checklist of practices to consider and a calibration of strengths and weaknesses. *All too often we use benchmarking to 'beat each other up', yet with a change in perspective we can use benchmarking to **help** each other up.*

After a significant merger, the Operations Excellence initiative in BP was established to encourage sharing, not only between busi-

Creating a common language is a basis for sharing

nesses of similar type (refineries, or manufacturing operations for example), but also across operations of different character. Underpinning this was a belief that the key principles of managing operations are actually common, regardless of whether the business is producing oil from a platform in the North Sea, or a factory producing polyethylene in Asia.

Building a self-assessment framework

BP's operating businesses are scattered around the world. Each believed its own situation was unique and therefore required special procedures. How then could we take an idea that saved the company money in one site and apply it elsewhere? When people from different parts of the company were brought together to learn how to improve reliability of their equipment they struggled to understand one another. They used the different words to mean the same things and the same words to mean different things. Look at the trouble we get into using the phrase *knowledge management* for instance!

A diverse team of operations staff representative of all of the operating environments came together for several days to create a common language. They first worked to establish a common set of practices, and ended up with 25 in total – common to *all* operations throughout BP. These were the areas they felt were important enough to define and measure consistently. Additionally, these areas were inclusive – relevant across all aspects of the operations, whether producing oil from a reservoir, refining it, or manufacturing polymers.

Examples of these practices include:

- raising morale and motivation,

- managing energy efficiency,

- forecasting production, and

- managing greenhouse gas emissions.

The full list of 25 practices is included as Appendix B. The starting point was a lot fewer than these 25. In refining, they were convinced only two mattered: reliability of equipment and reducing costs. But then others introduced more – such as health and safety, good communications, and dealing with unplanned breakdowns. Each was debated and included once everyone saw it was a common practice. In the dialogue some were grouped together and others split into two practices.

Having established these common areas of focus, and drawing on expert help where necessary, the team designed five levels of competence starting with level 1 being a very basic level to level 5 being a description of world-class performance. The group worked on a set of five statements each level being slightly higher than the last. Usually each had two or three variables. Let's have a look at one so we can explain.

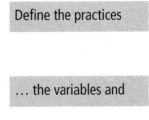

Define the practices

... the variables and

Here is an example element: reward and recognition

- *Level 5: all staff feel their contributions are valued, recognized and rewarded.*
- *Level 4: most staff feel valued and appropriately recognized and rewarded as individuals and teams.*
- *Level 3: a reward and recognition system in place but inconsistently applied.*
- *Level 2: people see little connection between performance and reward.*
- *Level 1: people feel victimized and blamed.*

... the levels of competence

The variables in this case are 'connection between performance and reward', 'how consistently is it applied', and 'how does it make staff feel?'

Scoring of these levels is subjective, the key aim is to encourage a conversation to gain consensus on how competent the group is at rewarding and recognizing people and where they need to improve.

Think about the practices that you need in your organization and who is strongest and who needs to build competence. What might it tell you?

- 'Who is good at customer retention?'

- 'Who is best at office relocation?'

- 'Who is best in class at quality control?'

- 'Who could make the best use of our good practice in call centre efficiency?'

- 'Who builds the best teams?'

Build, test and freeze

After sharing the framework of 25 practices and five levels of competence with others, there were suggestions for improvement, people disagreed whether level 4 was higher or lower than level 3 and a few sites took it and scored themselves to try it out. We gave it to a technical writer to improve the style and the language, but this did not work as our operations staff didn't recognize the language! After a month we were not progressing so we froze the self-assessment framework. It was not perfect but it was good enough to create a conversation at our operational sites with a common language.

We froze the framework but offered to collect suggestions for improvement based on their experience of using the self-assessment. A year later we reviewed the framework and made some changes. We benchmarked some of our level five descriptions by offering that part of the tool to good practice companies in other sectors. As a rule of thumb we agreed to make no more than 20% changes. We wanted to improve the self-assessment tool but we also wanted each site to be able to measure their improvement between assessments.

Using the self-assessment framework to create a dialogue

The biggest debate we had was how to ensure that sites scored themselves honestly and accurately. The breakthrough came by letting go control of the scores. The key aim is to encourage a conversation by the site about its strengths and where it needs to improve. By giving the site the freedom to assess their own competence in a number of practices and determine where they wanted to improve, they had the energy, the commitment to share and learn. What we learned was that once peer groups started sharing, they provided a greater challenge to their peers about levels of competence. If a site had generously scored themselves level 5 for a practice, then having to explain to their peers what they did to achieve that level was a good reality check. And people took it better from their peers than from a manager or an external consultant.

Rather like skills competence matrices for individuals it depends how the framework is used. If someone does their own assessment of their strengths and weaknesses they can determine what skills they want to improve to suit their development aspirations and the resources and opportunities available. If on the other hand the supervisor determines the strengths and weaknesses and tells the individual to attend a course, on report writing say, the individual may well attend the training but may not be committed to the outcome, they may just feel criticized.

> Self-assessment creates the commitment to learn

The assessment tool was offered to all one hundred operating businesses to run for themselves as a self-assessment. Typically, at each site, the operations manager would draw together a group of ten to twenty people – a diagonal slice through their organization – and the group would discuss and agree which of the statements was most appropriate to their site. A facilitator was available to help the conversation flow. It created disagreements, some felt they were less competent from their perspective than others did. Each was encouraged to

> Use a cross-section of people for diverse perspectives

give a specific example to illustrate their view. That helped the group reach consensus and also provide clues as to what they might do to improve. They arrived at an overall score for each practice – *'We are level 3 for managing greenhouse gases'* – for example. The facilitator was instructed not to allow halves; just round down and that will soon stop the practice!

Knowledge-based benchmarking

In addition to stating their current position, the team were encouraged to prioritize three practices they planned to improve during the next one or two years, and by how much.

'We are currently level three for managing greenhouse gases, and have set a target of level 5 by end 2002' would be an example of this.

They could select the practices according to which practice would have the greatest impact on their business and which they had the resources to cope with. We asked businesses to *set their own priorities* and record their own targets for improvement. For example, one of our chemical manufacturing plants in America had a low score (1 out of 5, based on the assessment tool) for their ability to manage corrosion. Based on that data alone, you might anticipate that they have a local problem with corrosion. When that same factory recorded their target score as level 1, it became apparent that corrosion management isn't a business priority for them. The reality is that the factory in question makes a polymer product using a non-corrosive process, and experiences favourable weather conditions – corrosion simply isn't a big issue for them.

So that was it. Every operating business worked through the self-assessment and recorded two sets of scores – where they are today, and where they plan to be in two years time. We captured these scores via an intranet Web site. Having identified some gaps in their performance, the business would agree some specific targets relating to closing these gaps, and spend the remainder of the year actively working towards those targets.

The river diagram and stairs diagram – visualizing the results

One of the most effective ways of creating an appetite for learning was by offering a picture of results. They say a picture is worth a thousand words. A picture that illustrates at a glance how a company's operations are performing can be worth millions of dollars. We made a breakthrough in helping the organization learn while doing by devising a simple yet illustrative picture.

A common way of visualizing performance

Having a *common* set of assessment measures across all of our hundred business operations enabled us to create exactly that picture. The picture portrayed the range of scores against all of the practice areas that we had defined, and could be used as a backdrop against which any single business could measure itself. By referring to the picture the whole team could see the areas it performed well in, and areas where others were better. This is the first step towards asking for and receiving help.

Like the assessment matrix, the vertical axis was calibrated from level 1 (basic competence) to 5 (world-class competence). The horizontal axis listed the various practices, side by side.

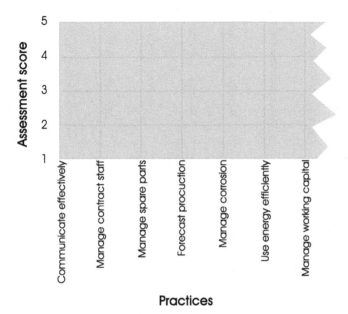

> Everyone has
> something to
> share, everyone has
> something to learn

Having completed the self-assessment, any business could see its current competence scores laid out against this framework – a unique 'heartbeat trace' which represented their competence. What people were often surprised about was that their strengths and areas for improvement were different from others, and that everyone has something to share, everyone has something to learn. It hadn't occurred to them before.

When their target scores were overlaid on this chart, the gaps between current competence and target competence became very clear, providing the managers of that business with some areas for focus. It was also clear whether there were other businesses already at a higher level of competence.

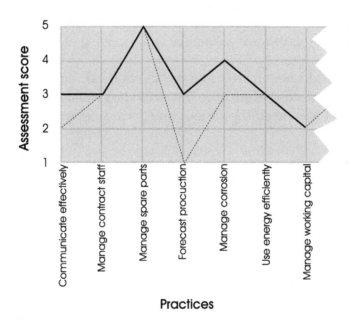

A strategic planning tool

When we aggregated the scores for all businesses, we saw some common trends. For example, not one of the hundred operational businesses reported world-class (level 5) performance in the areas entitled 'Communicate effectively' and 'Manage greenhouse gas emissions'. This was of particular concern to

the Head of Operations and to those running BP's environmental programmes.

Conversely, no businesses reported low performance in the areas of 'Forecast production' or 'Assure product quality'. We created a single picture that aggregated all the individual scores to illustrate these trends. We entitled the picture the 'river diagram'.

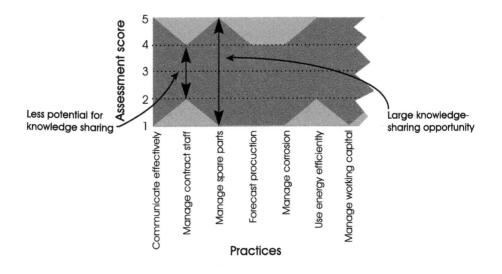

The boundaries of the river represent the maximum and minimum scores that any business reported. The 'banks' of the river are those areas mentioned earlier, where no businesses reported a score. The presence of a 'south bank' indicated competence inside the company (everyone at level 2 or above). The presence of a 'north bank' (no one at level 5) pointed us towards external benchmarks rather than internal examples, as we lacked sufficiently high competence inside the company.

A vehicle for knowledge exchange

Significantly, from a knowledge perspective, the width of the river at any single point gave a clear indication of the potential for sharing and learning in BP, of knowledge not evenly distributed. Where the river was narrow ('Manage contract staff', in the example above), most businesses were of similar competence, and there was less opportunity to learn from each other. Where the river was widest ('Manage spare parts', in this case) indicated a wide mix of competence, tremendous opportunities for sharing, and improving competence exist.

> Where the river is widest, you'll find opportunities for sharing

We were particularly interested in the wide points of the river because *suddenly, staring us in the face was a picture that showed us where to focus knowledge-sharing activities.* We encouraged and supported internal conferences, peer assists and the creation of knowledge assets on these topics.

The river diagrams proved to be a popular way to think about performance relative to the company as a whole. It would tell an operations manager how strong or weak their performance was relative to all others.

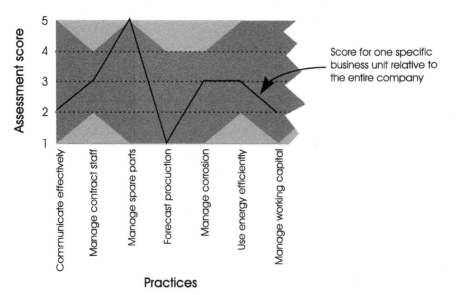

Score for one specific business unit relative to the entire company

Where are the gaps? Can you think of practices in your organization where there are large differences in competence, which when addressed would have a big impact on performance?

We created a process of common measurement of competence and the sharing of good practices across all of BP's operational sites. Having a common language and a common self-assessment tool for all operations is tremendously powerful, and enables sharing between previously unrelated businesses. We also coached the senior management, to ask questions such as, 'Who have you talked to in order to improve your operational performance?' and 'Who else can you share this with?'

Because we had divided the assessment tool into practices, we measured the scores for each practice. We consciously avoided summing the scores across the practices to get an absolute score for a refinery or a chemical factory. We weren't interested in absolute comparison – we wanted to share the details on a practice-by-practice basis. Because *everybody* is good at *something*, there are always some positive messages for each business. At a recent BP operations conference, a senior manager stated:

> '*We have world-class performance in almost every single practice – somewhere in the company. The trick is to recognize where it lies, and to apply it globally.*'

Identifying the knowledge to share and whom to share it with

The 'river diagram' stopped short of identifying who that operations manager could turn to for help.

> '*If I'm at level 3, who can I talk to who is at level 4 or 5?*'

This important question needed an answer, so we created a second picture linked to the first that revealed current and target scores for each practice – to provide a view for businesses that wanted to learn to identify who best to learn from.

Putting people in touch with people who can help

We found a simple, yet powerful way to represent these two axes – competence and priority – in a way that revealed which businesses had an appetite for learning, and whom they could learn from.

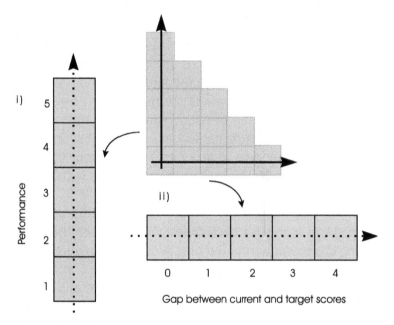

i) illustrates the performance axis
ii) is a measure of the appetite to improve that the business has for this particular issue – the size of the gap between the current score and the target score.

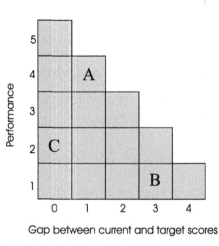

iii) Plotting both axes together leads to a 'set of stairs'.

Business A has a strong competence (4), and an 'improvement gap' of 1 unit – i.e. they aspire to reach level 5. Business B has a low competence at level 1, but an aggressive target to improve by 3 units – they aspire to reach level 4. Finally, Business C has a score of 2, but no improvement target – that particular practice is simply not a priority issue for them.

This mapping of competence against priority makes it easy for business B to identify the businesses from whom they could learn – business A in this case. Once we had populated a series of these 'stairs' with our one hundred businesses, we began to operate as a dating agency, and encouraged meetings, workshops and peer assists that brought together the high performers with the businesses with the strongest desire to learn.

Connect those who know with those who want to learn

We found that different zones within the diagram indicated where the most powerful interactions lay – between those with high levels of competence and those with a strong demand for knowledge.

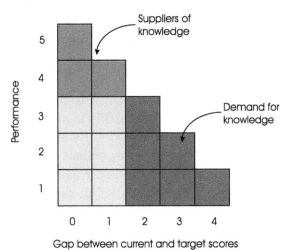

Gap between current and target scores

In summary, what could have been a simple table of competence which drove defensive and competitive behaviours into the company actually became a vehicle for knowledge sharing which acknowledged high-performing businesses, and encouraged others to seek out their help. There were some peer challenges to the relative positions of different businesses and that was healthy. After all the scores are only self-perceptions and led to a dialogue as to what was good practice.

When these important questions can be easily answered by *anyone*, knowledge sharing gets a fresh impetus.

> Would you like to try the river diagram for yourself? How about benchmarking you own knowledge management competence? Refer to the CD for an assessment tool and a customizable Excel-based model that generates the river and stairs diagrams.

So having designed it to work for operations in BP would it work elsewhere? Here's how Chris introduced it to Centrica.

Benchmarking 'customer management' in Centrica

At the heart of Centrica's strategy is their ability to create and maintain deep customer relationships – relationships which generate long-term value for the company.

In the autumn of 2002, Centrica decided to undertake a review of their customer management capability in order to understand the priorities for development and identify areas of good practice for knowledge sharing. An independent organization, QCi Ltd. was engaged to undertake an audit using their Customer Management Assessment Tool (CMAT™). This gave Centrica benchmarking relative to external companies, as well as its component brand units.

The CMAT™ assessment process involves the whole business and is essentially comprised of evidence-based interviews with key members of staff across and down the business: CMAT™ looks for evidence of joined-up thinking, asking such questions as:

- *'Do people at the front-line understand the vision?'*
- *'Do operations understand the customer proposition?'*

The findings from these interviews are then assimilated into the CMAT™ model and the business is scored across 260 detailed areas of activity, grouped into around 30 practice areas. Examples include: Measuring Channels, Managing Dissatisfaction and Understanding Competition. Finally, the CMAT™ results were inputs to the wider strategic planning processes within the brands and fed into action plans, with plans to repeat the measurement every 12-18 months and to track progress.

Emily Jacob, who coordinated the process from the centre, described the benefits as:

- Ongoing assessment of Customer Management capability - benchmarked externally and internally.

- Ability to refine plans and confirm still going in right direction - and to amend where not.

- Identify best practices for knowledge sharing within and between the brands.

- Identify gaps in knowledge/practice and opportunities to work together to collectively raise the bar in these areas.

- Ensures inputs to strategic planning processes are relevant and of priority.

Centrica uses the CMAT™ outputs as a fact base for understanding capability development priorities and learning opportunities, and for knowledge sharing opportunities. Emily continues:

The river diagram illustrates areas for sharing and improvement

'We use the river diagram to illustrate at a high level where good practice areas should be shared and where there are opportunities to make step changes in capability across the group. The results from the CMAT™ audits have enabled us to

*identify good practices for sharing and areas which require
greater focus across the brands. As a result, various projects
may "'spin-off" from the audit which in turn create more
knowledge for sharing across communities of interest, and
the capture of knowledge in specific areas. Group marketing
have used the intranet to promulgate this knowledge, and
are investigating other media such as CD-ROM, forums and
masterclasses.'*

Staff involvement with the CMAT™ process

Involvement in the CMAT™ assessments is on two levels. First of
all, there are those people who are interviewed as part of the
assessment process. This takes about 1.5 hours of their time and
they then will receive some feedback on the results they have
contributed to. Assessors will always try to give something back
to the interviewee before they leave the room.

Secondly Centrica will be conducting CMAT™ assessments using
a mix of internal and external assessors, with their own people
working alongside the QCi assessors. There is a robust accredita-
tion process for internal assessors to ensure the quality of the
benchmark database is maintained. For these individuals, being
part of the assessment process is an important part of their personal and professional development, as well as providing them
with a powerful network across Centrica's brand units.

For Centrica and its brand units, who will lead the process in
future, CMAT™ is fast becoming *the* framework by which they
understand what customer management is and what capabilities
are needed to execute it successfully. Emily concludes:

*'It is helping us to create a common understanding and a
common language surrounding customer management. It has
not happened overnight, but is a long process of stealth communications combined with the overt support of the executive
at the highest level: a combination of push and pull strategies
to ensure buy-in and active support of the strategy – and it has
helped awaken the knowledge-sharing culture that we need.'*

Centrica learned that using a river diagram can give a strong knowledge-sharing edge to a benchmarking assessment of customer management and is now applying it further, to its HR and project management processes.

Let's look now at a very different application of self-assessment and the river diagram – not to save money or customers – but to save lives in the worldwide fight against AIDS.

Creating the River of Life

The first thing that Geoff did on being seconded to the United Nations from BP was to visit Thailand with Dr. Jean-Louis Lamboray. The University of Chiang Mai had organized a meeting as part of their AIDS Education Programme on the topic of 'Participatory Learning from Local Response'. Jean-Louis Lamboray brought with him the ideals of AIDS Competence which he had experienced living in a community in Northern Thailand. Ian Campbell from the Salvation Army brought his experience of the facilitation tools used in Human Capacity Development. And Geoff brought his experience with the tools developed within BP to facilitate the sharing of knowledge.

The question was: how could this diverse set of experiences be brought together to create something more powerful?

> '... we had a different set of perspectives, we'd operated in different sectors ... when we had shared these we had a rich set of experiences and we could start to talk about possibilities ...'

One evening, after they had finished their formal sessions for the day, the group was in the hotel lobby having a drink. Geoff opened his laptop and showed the river diagram to Ian Campbell. Jean-Louis describes what happened ...

> 'Ian looks at the diagram listens a bit and says   The River of Life
> "We need this. This is the River of Life." The

River of Life turns out to be the logo of a programme on Human Capacity Development which Ian had been involved in with the Salvation Army in Africa. At that moment, there was a coming together of forces. Everyone saw the possibility at the same time. Everyone could see the practical use for the tool, how it could be adapted so that people could assess for themselves their level of competence in responding to HIV/ AIDS. It would give them a way to find out what they were good at and where they need to improve.'

Upon their return to Geneva, the team sketched out 16 practices that might contribute to being 'AIDS Competent', together with ideas for a set of five steps that would lead to AIDS Competence in each practice. This first self-assessment for AIDS Competence was sent to the University of Chiang Mai who tested it with local communities and provided encouraging feedback within just seven days.

The words, the language and the practices evolved for three months, based on the experience of the communities using it. Although there were still many different viewpoints, the group in Geneva decided to freeze the matrix at 10 practices in May 2003 for a year. They felt that the matrix had stopped progressing and changes were moving backwards and forwards over the same points. By stabilizing the assessment there is a valid basis for comparison and for learning between different countries, organizations and communities.

Sharing can occur at multiple levels

Once different communities had completed the self-assessment, they then had the opportunity to share their strengths and what they wanted to know. This has taken place on a local scale (e.g. villages within a particular region), where the opportunities for sharing are obvious and immediate. Workshops in Brazil and Lyon, France show that the sharing can work at a national and a global level and that these can be extraordinarily powerful and positive events.

The river diagram indicates that there are people out there from whom you can learn. The stairs diagram goes one step further and tells you who those people are. So if I am at Level 3, *who are the people who are at Level 4 or Level 5?*

When it comes to building AIDS competence, Jean-Louis believes that the lack of local ownership – ownership of both the issue and the solution – is the critical, often missing element. Self-assessment is an instrument for increasing awareness and then ownership of the problem, because it opens up a dialogue on each issue; locally, nationally, internationally within or between organizations.

> *'What we are seeing today is that the response to AIDS is frag-mented. People run with pieces. I'm doing women. I'm doing kids. I'm doing orphans. I'm doing Anti-Retroviral Therapy. But this method helps you to put whatever you are doing in the broader context of all that needs to be done on AIDS. This is a method to bring everybody together to assess what the priorities are.'*
>
> Jean-Louis Lamboray

So what are the lessons from using self-assessment and the river diagram, whether in BP, in Centrica or in the fight against AIDS?

- It can be used in several ways – as a strategic planning tool, to benchmark current strengths and weaknesses, to encourage target setting and measuring progress, and as a vehicle for knowledge exchange.

- It makes the connection between benchmarking and sharing knowledge – knowledge-based benchmarking.

- We can only share knowledge once we agree a common language.

- Be prepared to 'freeze' the assessment – get on with discussing the practices and not the framework.

- Creating the self-assessment is part of the process of deter-mining what's important and what the common language is. Ensure that you involve all the stakeholders.

- Encourage people to assess their own situation and to come together to share their results. They are more likely to determine and implement their own solution. Self-assess-ment is usually more empowering than an 'audit'.

- Knowledge is not evenly distributed. Where the river is at its widest there is the greatest potential to share and get everyone up to the same level of competence.

- Everyone has something to share, everyone has something to learn. Encourage people to talk about their own experi-ences, rather than about theories. Sharing what you know helps build self-esteem, and people are more receptive to learning from people who talk about their own situation.

We've figured out what knowledge we have to offer and what we want to learn. Let's look now at some techniques to encour-age the sharing.

Learning From Your Peers – Somebody Has Already Done It

Chapter Seven

In this chapter we discuss:

- Setting up a meeting to get help from others.

- What is involved in a peer-assist meeting?

- Who do you invite?

- Some examples of peer assist in use:

  – in BP

  – tackling AIDS in cities

  – 'rolling peer assists' for use with large groups

  – a potent weapon for an Afghan commander

  – relocating premises at the BBC.

It was just after Christmas and I was getting round to thinking about my holidays for the coming year, when Clive came for dinner. He brought with him some photos of a walking holiday in the Pyrenees. He had obviously enjoyed it and went through in great detail how the holiday company transported his luggage, how he had met up with the same people each breakfast and evening for a meal, and how the hotels were warm and friendly. During the day he was alone on the hills with a friend, but walking a given route so people knew where he was.

I explained what our situation was, that the children were going to 'do their own thing', and that for the first time my wife and I could choose to do what we wanted. Clive sent us the holiday brochure he had used and explained the ranking system for difficulty of walk. We also talked with a friend who had done a walking holiday and learned what she had found useful and what she would avoid another time. I sat down with my wife and we analysed what we had heard and what we thought was right for us. We selected a two-boot (moderately energetic!) holiday in the Jura region of France in May. We shared what we had chosen with Clive and our friend. They were pleased we had used their advice.

We thoroughly enjoyed our holiday. Without Clive's visit we may have spent it on a conventional package tour to Greece. We adapted what we had learned to ensure that we had a holiday that was right for us and different from normal.

What is a peer assist?

Sharing experience, insights and knowledge

Stated simply, a peer assist is a meeting or workshop where people are invited from other organizations and groups to share their experience, insights and knowledge with a team who have requested some help early on in a piece of work. A peer assist is all about a team asking for help, and it is for their benefit. Somewhere within BP, a peer assist is happening every week.

A peer assist:

- targets a specific technical or commercial challenge;

- gains assistance and insights from people outside the team;

- identifies possible approaches and new lines of inquiry;

- promotes sharing of learning with each other; and

- develops strong networks amongst people involved.

Not quite what you expected? In BP a peer assist is distinctly different from processes such as peer review and from bench-marking.

Peer review is perhaps a more familiar process in science and medical settings. It is also used in BP at the end of a stage of a project where decisions need to be taken. Peers provide assurance and challenge to make sure all relevant evidence has been taken account of and that tests are repeatable before proceeding to the next phase.

Benchmarking is information usually collected by a third party, measuring performance achievements and process. Benchmarking can make us aware of what has already been achieved by someone else, and usually comes accompanied

Has someone already done what you are about to do?

with 'best practices', a record of the process for those best achievements. The focus is generally on the practice or process, too often though that practice is not transferable and slavishly adopting that practice could, and has lead to, worse results. Peer assist concentrates on sharing experiences in different contexts, then working with those who have the experience to take the appropriate parts from several experiences to develop a 'fit for context' solution. Peer assist is a more collaborative process.

It's worth holding a peer assist when you are facing a challenge that you have not experienced before, where the knowledge and experience of others will really help, and when the potential benefits outweigh the cost of getting people together.

Here are some quotes from organizations that have used the process:

> '*I have just finished a peer assist where we saved the site something like $12-20 million and the company a number we are still trying to calculate.*'

> '*The power of the peer assist was not that it told us something we didn't know but rather that it got us into action to prevent us going down the same path as others.*'

> '*We realize we don't have to wait for an expert to tell us what to do, the knowledge is in this room.*'

> '*40 minutes later, the project manager from Pakistan had written down pages of ideas and suggestions that he planned to apply back home.*'

> '*A retail lubricants peer assist in South Africa saved £15 million in two days.*'

What is involved in a peer assist?

The concept of peer assist is quite simple and it is more than just sharing good practice. You notice we use the phrase good practice rather than best practice. Go to Chapter 12 to find out why. Experience and knowledge is gained in a particular situation or context. Knowledge is thus context-dependent and doesn't always transfer easily to a different context. So peers share their experience, both good and bad, and the context they gained it in and then take what is appropriate from all practices and develop a solution fit for the new context.

Let's look at a 2 × 2 matrix. We cannot go far wrong in a management book presenting a 2 × 2 matrix can we?!

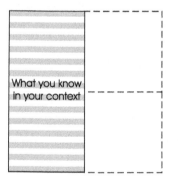

Having requested a peer assist, I share what I know based on the context in which I learned it. I don't force my best practice on others, because the reality is I have not done it any other way so I can't possibly judge what is best.

You then share what you know based on your context. Others also share their experience based on their own context, so the experiences and contexts will be diverse and the matrix multidimensional.

Together we learn what we all know, this is likely to be principles or processes that can be reused by others, and what we can learn from each other.

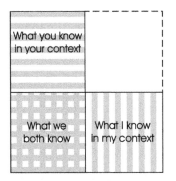

We are then in a position to work together to determine what is possible, either by adapting the practice to work in the new context or by creating something new from what we each know. So the emphasis here is on adapting practices to work for me or building something from the good parts of others' experience. This tackles one of the greatest barriers to knowledge transfer – the 'not invented here' syndrome. I am not *adopting* someone else's practice in a different context, rather we are *adapting* others' and I am making choices for my own context. Far less threatening to my ego and far more likely to be successful!

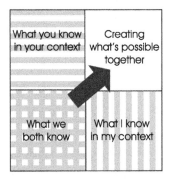

And from those possibilities we can take some action, either separately or together. Typically everyone leaves with a few things they can do differently, even those who only came to help! It is through taking new actions we create new knowledge. We test out a new approach and learn from that experience.

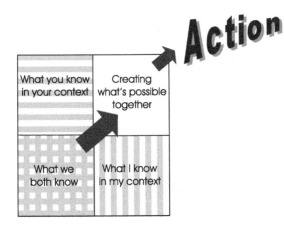

That is the essence of the peer-assist process. Want to try one?

12 steps to plan a peer assist

Several people have asked us how to go about planning a peer assist. There is no single right way to hold a peer assist, but here is a method that has worked well for us in a variety of settings. In BP, peer assists are usually held between graduates with a variety of international experience. It works for others too. Here's a starting point for steps to take – try it and then adapt it to your own context. Later in this chapter we'll share experience of others that have applied it using adaptations.

Facilitator's notes: participate in a peer assist that someone else facilitates before you facilitate one yourself. That way you'll have experienced the whole process.

There are 12 steps:

1   Clarify the purpose.

2   Check whether someone has already solved the problem.

3   Identify a facilitator.

4   Consider the timing and schedule a date.

5   Select a diverse group of participants.

6   Be clear about the desired deliverables and how you might achieve them.

7   Plan time for socializing to get to know each other.

8   Spend some time setting the environment.

9   Divide the time available into four parts, start with sharing information and context.

10   Encourage the visitors to ask what they need to know.

11   Analyse what you have heard.

12   Present the feedback, consider what each has learned, and who else might benefit. Agree actions and report progress.

Let's go through these steps in more detail.

Step 1 – Communicate a clear purpose

Peer assists work well when the purpose is clear and you communicate that purpose to participants.

Define the specific problem you are trying to get help with, consider whether a peer assist is the most appropriate process, then write a terms of reference. The self-assessment process described in Chapter 6 is one way to determine strengths and areas for improvement. Matching those who want to learn with those who already have strengths in the practice creates a great peer-assist topic, and identifies the likely participants.

It is possible to tackle complex issues where subgroups separate into different functions for detailed discussion after a common context session and then come together at the end to ensure plans are sympathetic. We suggest you start with something simpler though until you get comfortable with the approach.

Facilitator's notes: if you are the facilitator, get clear on the purpose of the peer assist and be sure that the person holding it genuinely wants to learn something. Ideally they are targeting the peer assist to address one of the key business risks. If the stated purpose is to gain endorsement or to get others to use 'my' method, then advise them that they require some other sort of meeting.

Step 2 – Has the problem already been solved?

Consider whether someone else has already solved the problem. Have a look at the organization's knowledge base to find out what others have already learned. Share your peer-assist plans with others. They may have similar needs, or relevant experience.

For example, several refineries held peer assists to improve cost savings. This involved some people repeating the exercise at many refineries in different parts of the world. A more efficient way might have been to hold a peer assist at a single refinery to identify cost reduction options for that particular refinery and extract the generic lessons for all refineries to adopt.

Step 3 – Get a facilitator

Identify a facilitator for the meeting external to the team. The role of the facilitator is to ensure that by managing the process the meeting participants reach the desired outcome. The facilitator may or may not record the event; make sure you agree roles beforehand. Plan the details of the peer assist in conjunction with the facilitator. Clarify the purpose and the desired outcome, and then plan the time to achieve that.

Step 4 – Timing is important

Schedule a date for the peer assist. Ensure it is early enough to do something different with what you have learned. Plan the peer assist early to make use of the help to deliver your business outcome. People frequently hold them too close to the decision date to make a real impact. Ask yourself 'If I get a result we do not expect, will I have time to do anything about it?' Give yourself time to apply the knowledge and be prepared for the unexpected. After all, you didn't invite people just to endorse your ideas. Did you?

> Will I have time to do something different?

Consider the timing, who is available on your selected dates, when are the holidays, in their location as well as yours? Invite people with enough notice so their diaries won't be full. Our experience is people can usually make it if you invite them at least a month in advance. And as soon as some have confirmed its amazing how others can change their appointments rather than miss it!

How long does a peer assist last? This depends on the complexity of the problem and the familiarity of the team with the context. Our experience has been that the majority of peer assists are one-and-a-half to two days long, though something useful can be exchanged in half a day.

Step 5 – Select the participants

Once the purpose is clear, develop a list of potential participants who have the diversity of skills, competencies and experience needed for the peer assist. Go to Chapter 10 p. 171 for further insights on picking the right help.

In the first edition we suggested meeting with 6 to 8 people is ideal, and we do hold peer assists with that number. More frequently now we hold them with larger groups of up to 50 people. These have been equally successful and a benefit is that more people have shared the knowledge. What is important for these larger groups is that everyone has a chance to voice their experience and ideas. Break larger groups into smaller ones to enable this.

Facilitator's notes: watch for the balance between the visitors and the home team. Avoid the urge to invite the whole project team into the meeting. It's easy to overwhelm the visitors and stifle new thinking.

Step 6 – Be clear about the deliverables

Be clear about the desired deliverables of the peer assist, and then plan the time to achieve them. Prepare carefully; optimize the time spent together so that you make use of the knowledge gained. The deliverables should comprise options and insights rather than the answer. It is up to the person who asked for the assistance to decide upon the actions.

Provide the participants with any briefing materials early enough for them to review them prior to the actual peer assist. This will help set the context and reduce the presentation time on the day, making more time for sharing.

Be clear in articulating both the objective of the peer assist and the business problem or challenge for which you are asking the group to provide input. Be prepared for these to be 'reframed' in the course of the challenge.

What do we mean by reframe the challenge? The problem you have identified might well be the symptom rather than the root cause.

Let's look at an example.

I attended a peer assist where the business manager was looking for some insights and options to make his gas project a more attractive investment. In setting the context, the focus was on the months of work that his engineering team had undertaken to take out unnecessary costs. This included investigating imaginative ways to use less material, to reduce the construction cost, and to defer costs until some gas, and hence money, was flowing.

What might they have forgotten? Would the combined brainpower of their peers come up with a solution based on their own experiences of large projects?

Be prepared to see the world through fresh eyes

After checking they understood the issues, the peers started talking about their own experiences. Viewing the problem for the first time, they rapidly came up with a number of alternatives. One option provided the breakthrough.

The focus of the business team had been on reducing costs. They wanted a better return on investment before they committed to spend the large amounts of money required. One way of doing this was to reduce the costs. What if they focused instead on getting a better return? Returns on investment were constrained by the terms of the contract with the government in which they were working, as the business manager had been told by the government not to discuss renegotiation. The experience of peers was that it was better to talk to the government early, discuss the problem and look for ways that both the company and the government could meet their objectives. After all, the country needed the money from royalties every bit as much as BP needed an acceptable return on investment.

The next day the business manager called his contact in the government to arrange a meeting. Thereafter the balance of activity shifted from engineering to contract negotiations.

Fresh eyes often see the world through different lenses and help you focus on the root cause. Fresh eyes reorder our assumptions. It can help us see what we already know in a new light.

Bill Isaacs in his book *Dialogue and the Art of Thinking Together* tells us:

> '*The intention of dialogue is to reach a new understanding and in doing so form a totally new basis from which to think and act. Dialogue opens possibilities and options, evokes insights, and reorders our knowledge – especially assumptions.*'

Peers by their questions often illuminate assumptions you did not know you were making.

Now you have completed the planning, you're about 60% of the way there. Well done! Grab yourself a coffee, go back to your desk and put your feet up for five minutes!

Step 7 – Ensure that the team socialize

Allow time in the agenda for the team to get to know one another. The team needs to socialize; this may be a dinner the night before, a walk in the park together, or half an hour over coffee at the start of the day; something to start building rapport. Remember, this is a temporary but newly-formed team. For the group to work openly together, to make and receive challenges, to have pet projects put under the microscope, it is important that people get to know each other. If you cannot manage this, plan dinner for the evening between the two days. It is amazing how much knowledge is transferred over a glass of wine and a good meal! One team started by sharing a communal Japanese bath together. But this is not absolutely essential to ensure a successful peer assist!

Step 8 – Define the purpose and lay the ground rules

So that's all the preparation what about the meeting itself?

Spend some time setting the environment and stating expected behaviours. If it's useful, use the matrix diagram on p. 103 to explain the sharing of knowledge. Brief the host team to listen actively, listen in order to understand and to seek opportunities. A defensive reaction can deter the visitors from offering further insights.

Design the day ensuring plenty of opportunity to reflect. We achieve this by asking a few simple questions.

The role of the peer assist participants is to offer help, know-how and experience to resolve the challenge without adding to the workload. However, some contention will raise the level of discussion. This will not occur if the group is being too polite.

Facilitator notes: ensure that the contention is focused on the activity rather than the person, and encourage people to consider alternative ways of completing the action.

Participants should recommend what the host team should stop doing as well as what extra they might do. Their time is limited, it's about prioritizing and focusing their effort onto the things that will make a difference.

Step 9 – Start by sharing information and context

Most of the peer assists we have been involved with last one-and-a-half to two days. Divide the meeting time into four roughly equal parts. Clearly articulate the purpose of bringing the peer-assist team together and make a clear request of the team. During the first quarter, get the resident team to present the context, the history and the plans for the future. Resist the temptation of having too many from the home team, and

Ensure that the visitors have sufficient time to contribute

telling too much. You want only to say enough to get the peer-assist team started in the right direction. They can ask questions if they want to know more.

The visitors have travelled and have given up some of their precious time to help you. Listen to what they have to say. There was one peer assist in London to which an engineer from Trinidad had been invited. He had travelled overnight for ten hours to help, but despite the facilitator's efforts to involve him, he wasn't given the space to say what he thought of their plans.

Facilitator notes: keep context presentations short and sharp. There is a noticeable tendency for any information presented becoming the focus of discussion. Avoid this by finding out what the visitors want to know.

Step 10 – Encourage the visitors to ask questions and give feedback

In the second part the visitors take up the baton. They consider what they have heard and discuss 'what they have learned that has surprised them', and 'what they haven't heard that they expected to'. The home team should take a back seat at this stage and maybe even exit the room. The peer-assist team then decide their course of action. What else do they need to know and whom do they know who knows? It may be that you want to talk to others to get their viewpoints at this stage, to talk to operational people or experts, customers or government officials. Set up some interviews, or make telephone or videoconference calls. Get views from contractors, external bodies or local staff if relevant. Request data and reports. What do you need to know to address the problem at hand? Remember it's not the job of the peer-assist team to solve it but to offer some options and insights based on their unique experiences.

Facilitator's notes: feedback is an essential part of the learning process. Allow time at the end of each day for feedback. Use an After Action Review (see Chapter 8, Learning Whilst Doing, p. 131) if appropriate to help set the direction for the follow-ing day.

Step 11 – Analyse what you have heard

The third part of the meeting is for analysing and reflecting on what you have learned. By all means involve a couple of the home team but make sure they don't close off options too quickly or drive towards their preferred outcome. They should be there to listen and learn. At this stage you are examining options.

Towards the end of this phase create a presentation to give to the wider home team. What have you learned, what options do you see and what has worked elsewhere? Tell the story of how it has worked elsewhere rather than 'you ought to ...'

We find storyboarding one useful technique here (see Appendix A).

Step 12 – Present the feedback and agree on actions

The last step for the visitors is to present their feedback to the team and to answer questions. Avoid getting into debate at this stage. As in all feedback, start with what has been done well and then what options there are to do things differently. Focus on the activity rather than the people. Finish with a general positive statement. On the receiving end, don't expect a silver bullet, a single solution to all of your challenges, a sudden flash of inspiration that tells you your problems are solved. Frequently the home team feel nothing new has come up. Remember, the visitors are reflecting what they have been told, coupled with what they know in their context. Often they confirm what you are doing is right but may set your priorities somewhat differently, they may test and reset the assumptions that are inherent in your approach. The peer assist may increase

> Don't expect a silver bullet

your confidence to do something when there is a difficult decision to take.

The person who set up the peer assist should acknowledge the help and the time people have given up. She should also commit to when she will get back with an action list of what the team are going to do differently. She may decide to invite the peer assist team back for future help. The benefit of this would be that they would not need to learn the context again and the peers can gain satisfaction from remaining connected with the project.

Next have the visitors reflect for five minutes and then say what *they* have learned and what they will take away and apply. Learning is never one-way, although the peer assist may start out along those lines. Offer what you learn to others, and provide a contact name for follow-up discussions.

> Learning is never one way

Consider who else might benefit from the lessons learned and the best way of enabling this to happen. Share the lessons learned with these individuals. Provide contact names for follow-up discussions and progress reports. Reusing knowledge is a smart way to avoid duplicating effort. For tips on capturing what you have learned go to Chapter 12, Leveraging What We've Learned.

> Consider who else might benefit from knowing

Finally carry out an After Action Review (Chapter 8). Did the peer assist go according to plan? What was different and why was there a difference? And what can you learn from that?

Stop and consider for a moment. Has someone already done something like you are about to do? Could you apply the peer assist process to a piece of work that you have just started, or plan to start shortly? Why not use the 12 steps in the resources section to plan your own peer assist? (See p. 300.)

Who are the right people to invite to a peer assist?

Lord Browne, the chief executive of BP, observed in a recent interview for *HBR* that:

'The politics accompanying hierarchies hamper the free exchange of knowledge. People are much more open with their peers. They are much more willing to share and to listen.'

He realized that the energy level in the room increased when he left the room. People started behaving naturally and sharing with their equals. Have you been in a meeting where someone is always trying to impress the boss, or where you have a reasonable question but you keep quiet because you don't want to look foolish in front of the boss.

So look across the hierarchy not up it. Make sure the participants are peers - peers can be more open, and challenge without being threatening. Ask the discipline head to suggest some names, so he or she is assured that the right challenge will be offered, but do not invite the discipline head to attend.

Go for diversity and avoid 'the usual suspects'

It's often the same people who turn up to help ('the usual suspects'). The risk is that no fresh ideas are circulated, and only the usual suspects become knowledgeable. Assemble a group of participants that have diverse skills and experience. Include people who will both challenge your mental models and offer options and new lines of inquiry. Diversity is important to ensure the proportion of common knowledge (the bottom left quadrant of the matrix) is not too large which could lead to 'group think' and limit the options for doing something different.

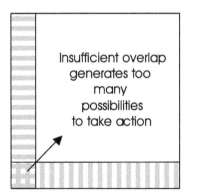

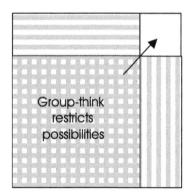

Let others decide whether they have something to contribute, rather than picking them. Consider including people from other disciplines, businesses, and organizations. When partners and external folks are involved this adds to the value of the assist. Why? The more experience from different context you can access the greater the number of dimensions with which to illuminate your problem. Small teams or syndicates (six to eight people) are more effective for working options.

But where will you find them if they are not to be the usual suspects?

At the simplest level it can be people working on different projects farther down your corridor. In a larger company, use a company yellow pages on the intranet (see Chapter 10, Finding the Right People). Or look elsewhere on the intranet for someone with the skills and experience to help you. If you don't have a knowledge directory or intranet then ask the head of the function to suggest some names, and use your personal networks

Secondly, make use of any functional networks. These have the knowledge to suggest who might bring something to your business or technical issue. It is, incidentally, a good way for individuals and teams to 'view and be viewed as a potential co-worker, without obligation' in case there is a vacancy in the future.

Consider posting an announcement of your peer assist well ahead of time. It will be worth looking to see if someone is already planning one on a similar topic. Perhaps you can join forces and help each other.

If you are working with a smaller organization, consider getting help externally. We have found that people love to help, and that they always learn something for themselves as a consequence. Generally, they are flattered to be asked.

OK, so now I know what a peer assist is, why and when to do it, what the steps are and whom I should invite. Let's give you some examples.

What topics?

Our first experience of a really good peer assist was a relatively low-key meeting called by a geologist before he wrote his project plan. As Steve observed, 'It's a common mistake for people to think, "We won't call them in until we have something concrete to show them; lets draw up our plans and bring people in to endorse them."' He invited people who were working on, or had completed, other projects in different parts of the world in a similar geological setting. He asked each of them to tell their story of how they had gone about their project. He asked them what had gone well, and what they would do differently if they did it over again. The group listed what was important in starting the geologist's project, given the different contextual setting. A facilitator captured the list of whats, whys and hows on a flip chart. This formed the basis for developing the project plan. The value of this meeting was in ensuring people spent their time working on the right things.

Developing the project plan

Here's another example. The context was that the project engineering team was about to spend a lot on some engineering design work before committing to construct the surface facilities to produce gas in the Sahara desert. The project team wanted to gain assurance that their plans were sound and that they had identified the key business and technical drivers to maximize the value of the project.

Is it the right project?

A collection of peers arrived from Aberdeen, Vietnam, Wytch Farm oilfield in southern England, and Trinidad. They were people running projects in different geographical locations, and at different stages of operation. They met with representatives from the project team the night before to have dinner together and to set the context and agree the purpose of the peer assist. As a result of this session the peer assist was reframed from, 'are we doing the project right?' to 'are we doing the right project given the business and political context?' and, 'is the pace right?'

The peers offered the following insights:

- They supported the engineering design work proposed since this clarified whether it was worth proceeding.

- They felt it was important to keep progress on the engineering project in step with all other parts, such as marketing.

- They had major concerns about aligning the company's needs with those of the National Oil company, who were partners in the project.

- They thought that the project team needed to clarify the prerequisites for making a positive decision to go ahead with construction.

- They pointed out that the strategy needed reviewing following the merger of BP with Amoco. The increased portfolio alters both the capital exposure and the impact on the country.

The project team agreed a number of actions, which they copied to the peers within two weeks of the meeting and subsequently pro-

Agree actions and report on progress

vided them with an update on progress. The business unit leader and the project manager took up the strategic issues.

This peer assist tackled the broader issues of identifying and shaping the right project as well as whether the project team were going about the project in the right way. For them, shaping the project to make the right investment was the foundation for assuring the project was being tackled correctly.

How have others adapted the process?

Cities have used it to share their response to the AIDS epidemic

An increasing number of cities around the world are taking ownership of the issue of HIV/AIDS and are confronting the growing threat. Municipal leaders realize that this issue is not just the responsibility of their medical services. They mobilize all stakeholders from civil society, from corporations and from various sectors of their municipal services. By building on their strengths, cities create a social transformation, where people are seen as the subjects of their own development rather than as the objects of institutional intervention. It is about appreciating and revealing local capacity to tackle a local problem. This process is universal; it applies equally to rich and poor cities, to low and high HIV-prevalence communities. By confronting AIDS, they build new experience in addressing local development challenges, and seek others' experience to build AIDS competence.

Seeking others experience to build AIDS competence

Thirteen cities with very diverse contexts met in Lyon in October 2003 to share good practices and experiences learned from local responses to AIDS: Bangkok, Curitiba, Durban, Gothenburg, Barcelona, Jinja, Kinshasa, Lyon, Mumbai, Ouagadougou, Parma, Port of Spain, and Simferopol. A team of three people represented each city, comprised of person living with HIV/AIDS, a representative of a local NGO (non-government organization such as a relief agency or charity) and a municipal official.

In advance of the workshop, all of the cities had assessed their capacity to respond to AIDS ('AIDS competence') by using a self-assessment tool. Through this self-assessment, municipal leaders stimulated a conversation between key individuals from civil society, businesses and the public sector to determine strengths and areas for improvement in their own 'AIDS competence'. The group set priorities for improvement; as a result, they knew what experiences they wanted to share, and what they wanted to learn from others. Offers included *'decentralizing HIV testing'* and the requests *'how to work with commercial sex workers'* and *'addressing vulnerable groups or situations'*.

They used the peer-assist process to share their experience on these topics, and identified the key advice others could use irrespective of context. This advice, supported by examples based on experience and references for more detail, constitute knowledge assets that others can reuse and build on. Moreover, the exchange between peers led to the identification of new possibilities for concrete action in their local context.

Participants used both the formal sessions and the informal time to learn much from each other on how to improve their city's response to HIV/AIDS. For instance Port of Spain offered to share its Stakeholder analysis methodology with Barcelona, Curitiba offered Brazil's experience on Access to Care to Port of Spain and Lyon learned from other cities what they did to detect HIV at an earlier stage. Durban asked for the help of other cities to achieve their goal of an AIDS-free generation by 2020.

Giving voice to experience

The self-assessment initiated, stimulated and nurtured the interaction between key groups in the response to AIDS via a peer-assist process.

> *'The tool has allowed us, in Ouagadougou, to see the need to take stock of our actions and to establish our priorities for the coming year'.*

The process is infectious. While dealing with a serious topic, several of the participants described the peer assist as a 'joyful time sharing knowledge' and all left enthused at the prospect of making a difference using their own local strengths. Mumbai will hold a workshop for their different local neighbourhoods first, then invite other Indian cities, and then the 'MegaCities network'. Curitiba is committed to a follow-up meeting in March of Brazilian cities following an initial successful workshop last August, and will invite Latin American cities to join. Jinja wants to present its experience to the 'Africities' meeting in Yaounde.

The process can be infectious!

The dialogue has just started. The participants recognized that the sharing does not stop at the end of the workshop and are committed to learning and sharing with each other. The exchange and capture of knowledge requires support. There are a number of tools and techniques already available to help facilitate this. All participants will be able to continue exchanging through the Local Response 'eWorkspace', using videoconferencing and they can use other external networks to maintain a community of practitioners.

Here's another example from the development sector.

Rolling peer assists

'KM4dev', is an online community of international development professionals who are interested in knowledge management issues and approaches. This group had a successful experience of peer assists when they helped a project manager from Pakistan. He had been very successful in organizing the local Pakistani community to come together to allocate people and financial resources, but locally elected officials felt undermined by the process. Within 40 minutes he had captured many pages of ideas and suggestions from the KM4dev community that he planned to apply.

Subsequently, at a KM4dev workshop in The Hague in November 2002 because there were more than 50 participants in the workshop, the group would have been too large for just one peer assist. The organizers were creative, and turned a problem into an opportunity. They thought that splitting the group into three smaller groups and having concurrent peer assists, then rotating after a certain period of time, would be a clever way of using the technique with a larger group. And everyone gets to hear each story and to contribute to it. It worked well and separate organizations have used it since then.

> Rotating peer assists give more people access to more stories

A number of organizations have used 'rotating peer assists' including the International Institute for Communications and Development, the Association of Universities and Colleges of Canada and the Canadian International Development Agency, with topics ranging from computer-enabled community development, promoting local ownership, adapting to major changes, promoting sustainability and effective program approaches.

What makes them different from a simple peer assist?

The person wanting help gets to tell their story multiple times. Each time they tell their story, they help themselves articulate and understand their challenge more clearly. Each telling enriches the teller's understanding.

As David Snowden says,

> 'We always know more than we can say, we can always say more than we can write down.'

Three different groups and consequently three different dynamics get a crack at helping to solve the problem. This provides fresh insight and increases the chance of innovation and alternative viewpoints. And the small size of the group increases the chance of people being heard.

Participants get to contribute to multiple stories. It increases the chances of them having relevant experience to contribute to one or more of the peer assists and of people seeing the value in peer assists.

It keeps the energy high in a workshop; and it gives them the chance to see a peer assist working in a number of different contexts. There is movement, people getting fresh stories, challenges, and insights.

What has KM4dev learned about holding successful rotating peer assists?

Allow sufficient but a relatively short time (25–40 minutes usually) for each peer assist round. It is possible to gather many different perspectives within a short timeframe and find quick solutions in a creative manner. Manage the time and direction of rotation well to keep things moving!

The more people identify with – and feel engaged by – the problems presented, the better the outcomes of the discussions. The issue brought forward by the peer assistee also needs to be concrete and linked to personal experience for better results. It should not be someone else's problem that is presented. It is important that someone is prepared to put their problem on the table, rather than presenting their 'best face' for the process to succeed. In order to do so the level of trust within the groups needs to be high. The facilitator plays an important role in creating a safe environment for the participants.

Facilitator notes: Summarize the suggestions succinctly, manage the flow of discussion, make sure all contributions are noted and heard, and ensure dominant participants don't monopolize or polarize the discussion.

A clear understanding of the process leads to successful rotating peer assists. It is important for the peer assistees, the peers and the facilitators to fully understand what is expected of them.

A concise presentation of the context and issue is essential, although on subsequent tellings the person will often rephrase their story based on peer questions and will be able to get to the point much more quickly, making appropriate solutions easier to identify.

The facilitator's role in recapping the comments of the previous round is also key. This enables the rotating peer-assist process to be an iterative one; it provides the opportunity to build on each other's ideas, moving from often general suggestions in round one to more refined solutions in rounds two and three.

Rotating peer assists are most successful when they are done in one room and everyone can see (on flip chart paper) what is going on, because people can 'see' what it looks like to share what they know – they get a sense of building momentum.

They recognize the value in sharing what they know because they can see people working together to identify insights/ideas to someone's problem (the flipchart also helps provide the visuals). They can see how their insights/ideas build on others to produce even better results for the peer assistee.

Facilitators' notes: Ensure there are enough flip charts and markers and have everyone write down what they hear or think!

The energy that is generated by the process has been known to lead to a form of competition, some groups wanting to 'outdo' the previous rounds in finding good solutions! If respectful of others people's ideas, it can be seen as healthy ...

Sometimes groups will try to outdo each other in offering assistance!

A potent weapon for an Afghan commander

The soldiers of the 3rd Brigade Combat Team, 25th Infantry Division (Light) are deploying to Afghanistan armed with a new and potent weapon – the knowledge of their predecessors.

Major Tony Burgess of the US Military Academy told us all about the CompanyCommand team introducing a new learning process in the army to connect company commanders who had served previously in Afghanistan with those who were preparing to serve there. CompanyCommand.com is the professional forum for army company commanders, connecting company commanders - present, past, and future - in an ongoing conversation about leadership. Their peer-assist strategy has three elements:

- to capture the knowledge of current and past commanders in Afghanistan in a booklet for future commanders;

- to bring together past and future commanders for face-to-face conversations about leadership in Afghanistan; and

- to create an online space within CompanyCommand.com focused specifically on command in Afghanistan.

First, they created the *Afghan Commander After Action Review Booklet* that detailed the lessons and experiences of 41 current and previous commanders in Afghanistan. Leveraging the network of CompanyCommand.com, they made a list of those who had served as company commanders in Afghanistan. They developed a Web-based survey that addressed issues relevant to company commanders, and then personally invited the past and current Afghan commanders to complete the survey. Finally, they compiled and formatted the responses into an 82-page booklet that one commander hailed as 'the best AAR I've ever read. We adjusted our training plan based on the draft version of this.'

After personally delivering the AAR booklets, the CompanyCommand Team facilitated face-to-face interaction between past and future company commanders of deployments to Afghanistan. They flew six officers who had commanded in Afghanistan to share with the commanders preparing to deploy, spending three days together poring over maps, talking about Afghan leaders and enemy tactics, and sharing ideas and experiences.

'This has been an invaluable experience,' said one Captain. 'The opportunity to hear actual stories and details rather than the usual "broad-stroke" generalizations really made the difference.'

Finally, the CompanyCommand Team created an online space for past, present, and future commanders in Afghanistan, so the conversations sparked by the booklet and seminars can continue virtually.

'There is no substitute for actual experience,' said Major Nate Allen, a leader of CompanyCommand.com. 'However, we can more effectively prepare for an upcoming experience by learning all we can from those who have already had the experience.'

By developing a peer-assist program that facilitated paper, personal, and virtual connections, they enabled peer commanders to learn from each other before deploying to combat.

And here's another one used for relocation too.

Moving from the studio to the Mailbox

The BBC employs some 27,000 staff who are located at many sites across the UK, Channel Islands and internationally. For example, there are 39 local radio sites in England alone. The relocation of staff to new premises and the refurbishment of existing properties is an ongoing and expensive task. This therefore seemed a natural place for the BBC's KM team to begin encouraging more effective sharing as it is a subject where:

- there is an extensive community of practice;

- the same tasks are often repeated in different physical locations – the knowledge is therefore highly transferable; and

- there is potential for huge cost savings due to the nature of the activity.

After a series of exploratory activities in Spring 2001, the BBC's KM team supported their first major 'Learn Before' session. The project team that requested the session were responsible for relocating BBC Scotland from Glasgow Broadcasting House to a new purpose-built premises at Pacific Quay, Glasgow.

The day long session involved over 20 attendees and was facilitated by a member of the KM team. In addition to the project team, people with experience of delivering projects of a similar scale from both inside and outside of the BBC were invited to share their experience. Two support assistants also attended; one to manage the audio recording of the entire session for transcription, one to take notes and then capture key learning points on video during the breaks.

The session was structured around three key areas of interest to the project team. For each agenda item, a series of questions were posed by the project team.

'We wanted everyone to feel comfortable and encouraged to contribute. However we also wanted the discussion to be structured and focused so that the best use was made of the time available. We held an informal discussion with the project team prior to the session to identify both their knowledge gaps and subjects where they felt a variety of perspectives would be beneficial. We then posed a number of broad but targeted "how to ..." questions and discussion points under each of the three agenda items. This worked well and helped the session flow.'

Tony Pilgrim from BBC's KM team

When facilitating the discussion, Tony used a simple framework for each agenda item to draw out stories and experiences from the contributors. In each case he simply asked:

1 What worked?

2 What didn't work?

3 What would you do differently in the future?

Using those three questions ensured that both positive and negative experiences were given equal value as learning points. Finally, asking what people might do differently in the future provided an opportunity for the group to brainstorm approaches to common challenges.

Following the session the learning was packaged as a knowledge asset. After approval from contributors and the project team it was published on the intranet. This enabled the project team to have a record of the learning shared and also provided access to the resource for the wider community of practice. The KM team ensured the asset was linked to relevant property- and project-orientated intranet sites and was searchable via the intranet search engine.

Since then, the published learning has been used by a number of other projects including the relocation of staff from Pebble Mill to the new Mailbox premises and the development of the new media village at White City in West London.

These examples should give you an idea of the range of topics that have been discussed at a peer assist and how the process has been used.

> You might consider trying the peer-assist process to tackle something you could use some help on – a bullying problem in a local school, or to develop ideas for fund-raising activities for your favourite charity. You don't have to limit yourself to workplace situations.

Summary

Here's a summary of what we have learned about peer assists over the last few years from these and other examples:

- Peer assists work well when the purpose or problem is clear and you communicate that purpose to participants. It should be a concrete issue that one or more participants are facing. Be prepared for the purpose to be reframed during the course of the meeting.

- Consider whether someone else has already solved the problem in which case you don't need to meet. Share your peer-assist plans with others. They may have similar needs.

- Ensure the peer assist is early enough to do something different with what you have learned. Ask yourself 'If I get a result we do not expect, will I have time to do anything about it?'

- Invite potential participants who have the diversity of skills, competencies and experience needed for the peer assist. Include people who will both challenge your mental models and offer options and new lines of inquiry.

- Listen for understanding and how you might improve your activity. Defending the status quo will not improve your project.

- Make sure all involved clearly understand the process and their role in it. The role of the peer-assist participants is to offer help, know-how and experience to resolve the challenge without adding to the workload. Get participants to recommend what the host team should stop doing, as well as what extra they might do.

- Consider holding a 'rotating peer assist' if the number of potential peers is high, and time is relatively short.

- At the end of the meeting, have each participant consider what they have learned and will apply from the peer assist. And ask them to consider who else might benefit from the learning.

- Finally, encourage the host team to share progress against the action list with the participants of the peer assist.

That completes the chapter on 'Learning before doing'. What other learning tools would you like to know about? The following two chapters cover 'Learning whilst doing' and 'Learning after doing'.

In this chapter:

- A simple process for continuous improvement.

- Why learning whilst doing is at the heart of a knowledge culture.

- How to introduce the discipline of reflection and learning.

- Who should participate.

Lessons from Lara Croft

Have you ever watched a child playing a video game and marvelled at how fast they learn? I find myself doing exactly that with my nine-year-old nephew, Simon. I watch transfixed as he weaves an impossible path through a jungle or labyrinth, cheating death by stopping exactly at the edge of each precipice, knowing exactly how far, when to jump, what to jump on and where all the bonus energy jewels and poison potions lie.

Perhaps this is all easier that it looks. 'Your turn uncle Chris!'

There goes my reputation for being the cool uncle - seventeen seconds of running, some of it backwards, and then straight down over the edge of the first canyon.

So how do they do it? I spend a fair proportion of my life working at a computer – I was doing it before Simon was born; yet
I'm the one who appears totally inept with JungleRaider III, or
whatever it was ...

How children learn continuously

It wasn't until I watched Simon tackle level sev-
enty-eight (it was a long game!) – the one that
he'd never tackled before, that things became
clearer.

'That wasn't supposed to happen' ... 'What if I try this?' ... 'There
was a jewel here in the last level' ... 'Supposing I jump up here
– oops. OK, up there then. Yeesssss!'

Once he was in new territory, he switched from remembering
the right sequence, to learning. Continuously learning, doing,
testing, checking, learning some more, until he cracked the
challenge, and then onto the next level.

The challenge for business world

That's the behaviour that is so often missing in
business. People are happy enough to remember the right sequence – to know the rules of
the game. People are happy to work on an
important project, and not 'come up for air' until the project
close-out. Sometimes, they need to be able to learn quickly,
and adapt in order to improve. It's not good enough to wait for
the end of the project for the review to draw out the lessons
learned, something needs to change now. Wouldn't it be great
if that sort of learning was routine in your organization?

Learning from the US Army – the After Action Review

For many years, the US Army has been applying
a short, sharp process known as an 'After Action
Review' (AAR) to improve their ability to learn in
the midst of action and improve teamworking.
One of the main drivers for this was their experiences in the Vietnam conflict.

At the peak of the conflict, it became apparent that foot soldiers
in the field had far more knowledge about what was going on

than headquarters. AARs were introduced to pass timely, relevant learning within and between teams of soldiers at times when waiting for a full evaluation report would mean waiting too long. To quote from the US Army handbook: *A Leader's Guide to After Action Reviews*, which is readily accessible on the Internet:

> *An after-action review (AAR) is a professional discussion of an event, focused on performance standards, that enables soldiers to discover for themselves what happened, why it happened, and how to sustain strengths and improve on weaknesses. It is a tool leaders and units can use to get maximum benefit from every mission or task. It provides:*
>
> - *candid insights into specific soldier, leader, and unit strengths and weaknesses from various perspectives;*
> - *feedback and insight critical to battle-focused training; and*
> - *details often lacking in evaluation reports alone.*

When do you hold an AAR?

A common misconception regarding AARs is that they should only be carried out at the end of a formal project or discrete piece of work. This is not the case. AARs are actually designed to aid team and individual learning *during* the work process and can be conducted after any identifiable event. An event can be either an entire small action or a discrete part of a larger action e.g. a shift handover, a project planning meeting, a key meeting or a visit to a community.

Using AARs during the work process, not after it

Perhaps you have recently commissioned for market research, or secured an important contract?

Perhaps you have just completed a series of interviews for a new recruit?

Events suitable for AARs simply have a beginning and an end, an identifiable purpose and some metrics on which performance can be measured (for learning after the project is complete, see Chapter 9 'Learning After Doing').

How do AARs work?

AARs are a simple way for individuals and teams to learn *immediately*, from both successes and failures, regardless of the length of the task in question. The learning is by the team, for the team. The format is very simple and quick – its a 'pencil and paper' or flip chart exercise. In an open and honest meeting, usually no longer than twenty minutes, each **Four simple questions** participant in the event answers four simple questions:

- What was supposed to happen?

- What actually happened?

- Why were there differences?

- What can we learn from that?

Team learning, and building trust, and team integrity are equal objectives of the process. Our experience was that the simplicity of the process and the low time requirements were key to its acceptance. To quote from a supervisor at Toledo Refinery in Ohio:

> 'There are times when you think "we don't have time to do this", then you do it and you think, "we don't have time not to do this."'

What a fantastic quote! We often struggle to break into peoples' routines when we introduce new initiatives, processes and ways of working because the burden is simply too great.

Let's try something before we go any further in this chapter.

Take a few minutes and reflect on something that you did yesterday. Can you imagine it? Can you remember what was said? How did you feel?

Now answer the four AAR questions:

- What was supposed to happen?

- What actually happened?

- Why were there differences?

- What can you learn from this?

What does that tell you about what you could do differently tomorrow?

That is what you can get from a small amount of personal reflection. Just imagine what a team could achieve by taking time out to reflect similarly on what they have achieved.

AARs are simple to remember and simple to use. Because of this ease of use, they became quickly adopted and implemented by operations staff at several different parts of our business. We used the following guidelines when introducing AARs to BP.

1 Hold the AAR immediately

AARs are carried out immediately whilst all of the participants are still available, and their memories are fresh. Learning can then be applied right away, even on the next day.

In BP Vietnam, AARs were held immediately after every meeting with the Vietnamese authorities, as a means of building up knowledge of the negotiation process.

> Reflect on what happened whilst the memories are fresh

'Each team had a fifteen minute debrief using the AAR format, after each discussion with the government. This was a very powerful tool within the team. They could look back at what they did, and change what they doing the next day.'

Bruce MacFarlane

Try and plan the AAR to fall within the allotted time for the event, so it doesn't appear as an add-on. Include it in the agenda of a meeting, rather than introducing it as an afterthought.

2   Create the right climate

The ideal climate for an AAR to be successful is one of openness and commitment to learning. AARs are learning events rather than critiques. They certainly should not be treated as personal performance evaluation.

There can only be one poor performer in an AAR: the one who is not candid about both things that went well and things that did not.

'Pin your stripes to the door'

Everyone in the event participates, and everyone is on equal footing. The US Army describe a notion of 'pinning your stripes to the door' – that is, everyone's view is equal – and within the construct of the AAR process, junior soldiers feel completely free to comment on and challenge the actions and instructions of senior staff.

This openness is seen as a vital part of the process of building team integrity. For this team integrity to flourish, there should no spectators, no management oversight – just participants who have earned their right to comment by being part of the action.

3   Appoint a facilitator

The facilitator of an AAR is not there to 'have' answers, but to help the team to 'learn' answers. People must be drawn out, both for their own learning and the group's learning. What you are trying to get to, is what the army call 'ground truth' and a facilitator should be able to guide the team to this point – navigating towards some of the unspoken issues.

> Facilitation is an important role for drawing out the learning

Sometimes, however, a facilitator is needed to set the climate of the meeting. The facilitator ensures the meeting is open and that blame is not brought in. He/she must also make sure the process is quick and simple, and owned by the participants. One of the key success factors in the AARs is that everyone has a chance to speak.

The following quote illustrates the power of this factor when working with a multicultural team:

> *'Generally the British are the only ones to speak, so facilitation of the AAR is crucial. I made them answer the AAR questions round the table. You have to try and make the team leader shut up! I got a Vietnamese or a Norwegian to answer the questions first. Obviously I couldn't facilitate all of the meetings, so I excused myself from the process. I said "AARs are for the people in the team, I am here to facilitate the conversation". I turned up to the AAR, and made sure the person leading the AAR was not the team leader. Then I pushed my chair as far back as I could, but ensured everyone had their say.'*
>
> Bruce MacFarlane

4 What was supposed to happen?

AARs are very straightforward. The facilitator starts by dividing the event into discrete activities, each of which had (or should have had) an identifiable objective and plan of action. The discussion begins with the first activity: 'what was supposed to happen?' An important discussion follows until all have shared their understanding of what was actually supposed to happen.

This is often the most revealing part of the process. Unless there was a clear, well-communicated and unambiguous objective and plan, then it is likely that different members of the team have different understandings of what was supposed to happen. In this event, a successful outcome is unlikely.

Facilitator's notes: try asking people to quickly write down their own personal understanding of what was supposed to happen on a scrap of paper. After a couple of minutes ask them to read it back to the group.

The question 'what was supposed to happen?' should be equivalent to 'what were the objectives of the activity?' For example, when reviewing a team meeting, 'what was supposed to happen?' may be better treated as 'to decide, and gain team buy-in, to the 2001 strategy', than dwelling on details such as 'we were supposed to start at 8.30, take a 15 minute break for coffee' etc.

5   What actually happened?

Understand the facts – not the opinions – about what really happened

This means the team must understand facts about what happened – the US Army refer to this as 'ground truth'. Nothing sobers an exaggerated view of an event more than one's own words or actions played back for all to see and hear. Remember, though, that 'ground truth' is there to identify a problem not a culprit.

Facilitator's notes: this part of the process is vital and can be contentious at times, as people move from theory into reality – don't rush it. Sometimes people will dwell on the mundane aspects of an event when there may be a deeper underlying issue that they find difficult to talk about as a team. If you can encourage one person to make a more personal disclosure about how they felt rather than simply what happened, it can have the effect of 'unblocking' the process, allowing more open exchange to occur. These first two questions establish the facts, challenge people if they start moving on to opinions, ask them to save them for the later questions.

6 Now compare the plan with reality

The real learning begins as the team compares the plan to what actually happened in reality and determines, 'why were there differences?' and 'what can we learn?' Typically, the responses to these two questions blur, but ensure all the major differences are expressed. Successes and shortfalls are identified and discussed. Action plans are then put in place to sustain the successes and to improve upon the shortfalls. We have used these after training courses and the learning is much richer than from a series of individual evaluation sheets. People learn something from the differences in perspectives of the others in the group.

Facilitator's notes: try asking people to quickly write down one key learning for themselves to take away from the meeting. Often the act of writing it down will help the participants focus on what's important and memorize the learning for future events. It may be necessary to question quite deeply during this section, repeating the question 'why was this?' in order to get to the underlying reasons.

> Set in place some actions to embed what has been learned

7 Recording an AAR

Recording the key elements of an AAR clarifies what happened and compares it to what was supposed to happen. It facilitates sharing of learning experiences within the team and provides the basis for a broader learning programme in the organization.

AARs generate summaries of learning points, which can have high value for the team. That value is often specific to the team in the particular context of the event being reviewed, hence in our experience, AARs are not shared widely - they are primarily learning for the team.

It is useful to capture a record of the AAR points and agreed actions to remind the team of the lessons that were identified. A typical example of this is a two-day meeting or workshop. At the close of day one, a participant conducts a fifteen-minute AAR on the outcomes of that day, and the learning points are captured on a flip chart. At the start of the second day, this flip chart is referred to by the team as a reminder, enabling them to build the lessons of the previous day into their current activity.

Facilitator's notes: the reality is that in most organizations there is a reluctance to share lessons beyond the immediate team, but there is a willingness to share the corrective actions taken. The key learning points from an AAR are valuable because they are timely – they represent things as they are today, rather than as the product of an audit report. For this reason, it is always worth asking the question: 'is there anyone else with whom we could share what we've learned.'

Power comes from simplicity

In introducing AARs to parts of BP, people were repeatedly struck by the simplicity of the four questions, and the fact that the US Army had institutionalized the process so effectively. One memorable photograph showed soldiers conducting an AAR (complete with flip charts!) in the jungle after a day's action. What possible excuse could a refinery operator or a team leader have for not creating the space for an AAR? Mitch Bowman from Toledo, Ohio is one such leader who rapidly saw the relevance of AARs to his refinery operations:

AARs any time, any place, anywhere ...

'This process saves a lot of money, big money. A lot of times guys see problems coming before the supervisors. And many won't say anything because it's not their job and no one asks. So the problems happen – there is downtime, big losses. The AAR lets those things come out, ahead of time, just because you're asking.'

Mitch Bowman

'Just because you're asking' – that is the key point. AARs create the space – just fifteen minutes of it – to ask the key questions.

One of the most powerful examples of After Action Reviews having an impact was in the construction of over one hundred retail sites – petrol filling stations – across Europe in 1997. BP worked with its contracting partner Bovis on this major project, and Bovis applied the AAR process after each activity. For example, pouring in the concrete foundations or setting up the pumps. These AARs captured timely lessons that could be applied immediately to the next retail site. By the time the construction programme was completed, Bovis acknowledged that learning tools like AARs had helped to reduce service station build time by two weeks and reduce the cost by five per cent.

The benefits – faster delivery and reduced costs

To make the army's learning philosophy more tangible, we enlisted the help of retired US Army Colonel, Ed Guthrie. There are times when the tacit knowledge bound up in a practitioner is far more valuable than any number of written facilitators guides, so we tracked down the 'real McCoy'.

Colonel Ed flew with us to several BP sites around the world and captured the imagination of even the most sceptical of engineers with his colourful war stories.

Would you like to hear Col.Guthrie for yourself? Check out the CD for a video clip of 'Real McCoy' Ed describing the After Action Review process first hand.

What struck home most to Keith, a member of the team who accompanied Ed to Scotland, was the sense of incompleteness that Ed felt if he hadn't conducted a personal AAR on his day's activities. Before the plane had left Edinburgh airport, Ed already had already produced a scrap of paper and started to ask those four important questions.

AARs as a personal learning tools

Although BP hasn't embedded After Action Reviews to the same extent as the army, they are widely used across their activities. Whether a refinery operations team, an internal workshop, or a meeting with contractors – every day, somewhere in the company those four questions are being asked.

- What was supposed to happen?

- What actually happened?

- Why was there a difference?

- What can we learn from that?

An After Action Review programme at the Debswana's Jwaneng diamond mine

Here's how AARs were applied to diamond mining recounted by Ian Corbett of De Beers and Nick Milton of Knoco Ltd.

AARs are a girl's best friend!

'Jwaneng, in Botswana, is the location of the richest diamond mine in the world. This single mine, operated by Debswana, a partnership between De Beers and the Government of Botswana, produces nearly a fifth of the world's diamond supply, and diamonds from Jwaneng and its three sister mines provides three quarters of the export earnings for Botswana. Both for De Beers and for Botswana (as well as for the buyers of engagement rings the world over) it is vital to keep this mine in production!

Part of the extraction process for diamonds involves passing the crushed rock over some screens for washing the rock and separating into different sizes. There are eight such screens at Jwaneng dense medium separation plant. These screens needed to be upgraded to double deck screens as part of the ongoing optimization process to improve processing capabilities. While they are being replaced, production throughput is reduced, and that means a loss of revenue as there are no diamonds coming through part of the circuit. So it is very important to be able to change the screens quickly and effectively.

In 2002, Debswana were in the early stages of introducing knowledge management. One of the tools they wished to try was the After Action Review. At first sight, the AAR looked almost too simple to be serious! But the ease of application appealed to the management team as a good place to start. Jwaneng was just coming up to a major screen change in the dense medium separation plant. A local KM team saw this as a good opportunity to try AARs. So after the first double-deck screen had been changed they brought together the client base, the contractors, and their own team, and they held an After Action Review.

The first screen change took 190 hours, but by capturing the lessons on how to do it better, and applying these lessons to the next screen, they were able to change it in 70 hours. The team were able to hold that performance for the next seven screens, and the collective value of the diamond production they otherwise would have lost was in the region of $1 million. It was a dramatic result, and not just in monetary terms. While the mine was very pleased with the financial impact of the AARs, management saw the positive impact on the hearts and minds of the team as being equally beneficial. The people were suddenly more engaged, energized, and lots of ideas began for flow. Suddenly lots of people were not only looking for opportunities to improve performance but also seeking ways to apply knowledge management in different aspects of their work.

By Nick Milton and Ian Corbett

Let's move on from the diamond mines of South Africa to the relief and support operations of international aid agency, Tearfund.

Learning Reviews in Tearfund

Learning Reviews are the most established tool for capturing knowledge at Tearfund, and have become a part of the culture through their simplicity and immediacy. Astrid Foxen, who heads up knowledge management, takes up the story:

> 'We started in one of the operational areas of Tearfund looking at the way we respond in a disaster situation. In 1998 floods hit Bangladesh and we asked the desk officer in our Asia team responsible for Tearfund's response to undertake a learning review with the key stakeholders. The next time a flood situation occurred in Orissa, India, the lessons learnt in Bangladesh were used to improve our response. It was important to try it in an area where the results of the review could be quickly seen.'

Learning Reviews at Tearfund cover a wide spectrum of events, ranging from an informal five minutes at the end of a team meeting to a formal all-day meeting. The simplicity of the 'What went well?' and 'What could have gone better?' questions mean that it is easily adaptable, and can be as quick or as long as you need to make it. Informal learning reviews are usually held within a team or cross organizational project team, usually at the end of a team meeting, and are facilitated by the team leader or a delegated member of the team. Formal Learning Reviews are distinct meetings with all the key participants of the event being reviewed. They are facilitated by a trained internal facilitator and a scribe, to ensure that all formal reviews have a written output that is held on the intranet.

Check the CD for an example of Tearfund's 'Learning Review' template.

Astrid continues:

> '*Staff are usually willing to participate in a learning review, and are able to see the benefit for their team and the organization, and also for themselves of sharing their learning and knowledge – it's one of our organizational values. When we started out it was at the suggestion of a member of the KM project team. The trigger is now the enthusiasm of our staff, and the belief in the effectiveness of the process of the event owner.*'

Lessons from BP, Tearfund and De Beers

- These are simple to do and quick to get results. The small time commitment can make AARs an 'easy sell'. They are common sense but not common practice.

- Look at the areas of your organization, and try out an AAR in areas where an activity is often repeated and where the benefit can be seen very clearly and quickly.

- The reflecting and learning together is more powerful than individual learning, it impacts hearts and minds and it builds high performing teams.

- As a facilitator, encourage and support team leaders – both as active listeners and leaders of reviews.

- Pro-formas and templates can help in the transfer of the methodology. It keeps people on track.

- What you learn and apply next time is valuable already, but think about how you are going to share the learning and knowledge gained through the reviews with others. This will not only leverage the benefits but is a positive advertisement for knowledge management.

- The discipline of always doing AARs pays big dividends. It is a powerful method of continuous improvement.

Of all the learning tools mentioned in this book, in our experience, AARs are the easiest tool to introduce. Because of this, they are a great place to start (See Chapter 5, Getting Started – Just Do It, p. 68), if you're looking for an entry point to introduce knowledge management to your organization.

But what about a tool to help reflection after a larger piece of work or a substantial project? Turn to the next chapter, Learning After Doing, When It's All Over, to learn more about the retrospect process.

Learning After Doing
– When it's All Over

Chapter Nine

At the close of a project or any substantial piece of work, it's worth taking a little time to reflect on what has happened, and to capture that for future use by others.

In this chapter we cover:

- A simple process for capturing and transferring lessons from any project or event.

- Detailed guidelines and tips for conducting a review.

- A method for getting to the root cause.

- Who should participate.

- The use of video interviews to enrich the capture.

- Application of the technique by BP, Tearfund and De Beers.

H ave you ever wondered what it must be like be a professional footballer immediately after a defeat? We see the deflated team trail dejectedly from the pitch ... but what happens next?

Learning from the football field

At primary school, the dressing rooms could be charged with stinging recriminations, egos were punctured as last week's hero became this week's villain.

> *'Six-five! Collison, you cost us the game – why didn't you pass the ball?'*

> *(Thinks) 'Six-five. Why didn't I pass the ball?'*

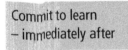
Commit to learn – immediately after

In professional circles, of course, things are somewhat different. The coach will bring together the team immediately after the match – those who have played and those on the bench who will play in future games. Together, they will go through a review of the game – the strategy, tactics, teamwork, the good and bad points. Together, they will watch videos, watch them again, review decisions and identify what they could have done differently, making a mental note to build this into future games – especially those against the victorious team this time.

So why is it that in business, all too often we slip into something closer to the primary school model?

Even when we do expend time and energy in reviewing a project, or a piece of work – the organization too often fails to take advantage of its own history.

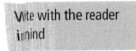
Write with the reader in mind

Our experience with project close-out reports and post-project appraisal write-ups is that they simply don't get read most of the time. Why is this? Somehow they don't seem to be written with the reader in mind. Somehow they lack timeliness, completeness, passion, even credibility, especially when they become a catalogue of reasons why 'it wasn't anyone's fault'.

According to Lord John Browne, in his 1997 *Harvard Business Review* article, 'Unleashing the Power of Learning':

'Most activities or tasks are not one-time events. Whether it's drilling a well or conducting a transaction at a service station, we do the same things repeatedly. Our philosophy is fairly simple: Every time we do something again, we should do it better than the last time'

That's exactly the philosophy that BP aspires to practice when drilling wells, acquiring companies or building a pipeline.

What is a retrospect?

In many parts of its business, BP has been using the process described as a *retrospect* as a tool for 'learning after doing'. A retrospect is a simple meeting, called after the completion of a significant piece of work – at the end of the war, rather than after one of the battles. Perhaps you have just completed a major product launch, a company reorganization, an acquisition or a two year development programme? A retrospect would be relevant in each case.

- It is a way to ensure that a project team feels 'complete'.

- It allows the team to truly understand what happened and why. Something like this will happen again, so let's take the time to understand what happened and why.

- It is a quick and effective way of capturing the knowledge before the team disbands, securing the lessons learned for the benefit of future project teams.

- It is a way of transferring lessons immediately to the next similar project, as it is about to start.

The retrospect meeting lasts from a couple of hours to a couple of days, and requires facilitation. In many ways, the structure resembles that of an AAR, and it is very reflective.

More in-depth than an AAR

- Revisit the objectives and deliverables of the project.

- Ask what went well. Ask 'why?' several times.

- Ask what could have gone better. Ask 'why?' several times.

However, unlike an After Action Review, a retrospect is conducted in more depth – taking anything between an hour for a simple project to up to two days for a complex partnership, involving several organizations.

The other significant difference is that a retrospect is a way for a team to reach 'completion' as well as for capturing lessons and insights for a future project. There are two distinct categories of projects – those projects that are repeated on an ongoing basis, such as drilling an oil well, and one-time projects that may not be repeated for five years. For the former there is likely to be a direct customer for the output of the meeting – indeed, if possible, that customer should be present to pick up the full richness and subtleties of the interactions – subtleties that the capture may well fail to pick up. For the other, a more thorough capture is required. BP took the time to do a retrospect after it had combined with Amoco to form BP Amoco. It wanted to develop its capacity for acquisitions and mergers. Within three years it had successfully acquired three other companies, Arco, Castrol and Aral.

Include the customer

Here are the specific steps and facilitator notes that have been successfully applied for over eight years in BP.

1 Call the meeting

It needs to be a face-to-face meeting. Videoconferencing can be used, it's better than nothing, but a physical meeting is generally more effective. If you are concerned that people will not be open at the meeting, you may also need to conduct one-on-one interviews to supplement this. Don't try and conduct a learning capture by e-mail!

Hold the meeting as soon as you can after the project ends, ideally within a couple of weeks. The team disperses, memories fade, and events become glossed-over if you leave it much longer, and the past can develop a rose-tinted hue.

Consider positioning the meeting as a celebration if appropriate – this experience from building retail sites in Japan illustrates the point:

Learning events can be celebrations!

> *'I guess it was successful because the event itself had been a success. It was a very upbeat meeting, so it wasn't seen as a witch-hunt. It was done within the spirit of a celebration – T-shirts were handed out!'*

Facilitator's notes: If possible, the venue for the meeting should be closely related to the work environment of the project itself. The project office or 'war-room' is ideal, as it will bring context flooding back for the team. Avoid neutral or hotel-based locations – this is about capturing the reality of what happened. Sterile hotel conference rooms can lead to sterile conversations!

As a rule of thumb, calculate the duration of the meeting allowing 20 minutes per person, or half an hour if it was a lengthy, contentious or complex project. Also:

- *Ensure that a variety of workshop materials (e.g. Post-it notes, flip charts) are available.*

- *Take a digital camera.*

- *Include a 'customer' for the lessons whenever possible.*

2 Invite the right people

If a similar project is due to start, or is already underway, then there is great value in the new project team attending, so the knowledge can be transferred in real time as soon as it is surfaced.

The project leader needs to attend, as do key members of the project team. Ideally, the project customer/sponsor/client will attend, at least for the first part of the meeting. However, there is a need to be sensitive to the presence of a highly-placed sponsor at the meeting – it may inhibit some team members.

Position the meeting correctly

Ask the project leader/coordinator/manager to schedule the meeting. He or she has most ownership, knows who needs to attend, and still probably retains some influence in the project team.

In the call to attendees, announce that the purpose of the meeting is to make future projects run more smoothly, by identifying the learning points from this project.

> If someone in your organization is about to start a piece of work similar to something that has been recently completed, why not suggest that they use a retrospect as a tool for drawing off the learning points? After all, they have a vested interest.

Below is an example invitation note for a retrospect on a key BP Chemicals acquisition – just prior to the merger with Amoco:

```
I am pleased to confirm the meeting 'Learning from
Styrenix' on 13th November in Antwerp.

The purchase of Styrenix was BP's largest acquisi-
tion in the Chemicals sector for almost twenty years.
Given BP's growth agenda it is possible there will
```

be further acquisitions. It is critical that we take note of the lessons from the integration so that any such future acquisitions have the benefit of what we have experienced and learnt. The BP–Amoco merger is the most immediate application where these lessons will be useful.

The Integration Steering Group asked that we prepare a thorough review of what has been learnt. To help us achieve this I have asked Chris Collison and Barry Smale of BP's Knowledge Management Team to lead us through a process in this one-day workshop.

You can find more information on the Knowledge Management team's work on retrospects (that's what they call what we'll be doing) on the intranet Web site http://gbc.bpweb.bp.com/km/Tools-techniques/retrospect.htm

More details will follow shortly.

Thanks again for agreeing to attend

Mike

Facilitator's notes: If members of a future project team are able to attend, then try to maximize the informal, social time. Split the meeting across two days with room for dinner and bar conversations. Enlarge the coffee breaks at key points in the day; you'll find that once in the same room, people simply cannot stop sharing.

3 Appoint a facilitator

Find a facilitator who was not closely involved in the project, to ensure the meeting concentrates on 'what should the next team do in similar circumstances' rather than on 'what we did'.

Independent facilitation is a must

If the facilitator is remote from the project, or the subject matter is complex, then she or he may need to do some preparation e.g. discussions with key players, more in order to understand the hot issues than to understand the content in detail.

The facilitator also needs to be outside the line-management structure, and the meeting needs to be clearly separate from any personal performance assessment.

Perhaps you're wondering where you might find a facilitator, or what the skills you might need to act as a facilitator yourself?

- Get the purpose agreed up front - the facilitator's role is to do whatever is necessary to help the team achieve this.

- Focus on the process rather than the content.

- Watch people's body language - it will tell you more than their words alone.

- Ensure a balanced contribution from all staff - ask questions of the quiet ones.

- Trust your instincts to ask the 'unasked questions'.

- Clarify distinctions between facts and opinions.

- If the purpose of the meeting is not achieved, ask 'what will you do next in order to achieve what you wanted?'

- Get the participants to focus on what actions they will take, rather than on what others will do.

It's about doing even better next time.

Facilitator's notes:

- *Ask people to introduce themselves and their role. This may feel like overkill for a project team who have been working together over a year, but it can be surprising what is discovered!*

- *Make sure the project team 'owns' the meeting. It's their meeting not yours, hence be prepared to compromise over meeting structure if necessary. The important thing is that all participants have an equal voice.*

- *Start the meeting by reiterating the purpose – this is not to assign blame or praise but to ensure future projects go even better than this one. Better still, have the project sponsor do this.*

- *Set an atmosphere of openness – if necessary you can introduce 'rules of the game'. There are no right or wrong answers. Affirm that no record of the discussion will be distributed without the agreement of all the participants. Names can always be dissociated from quotes if necessary.*

- *In a big meeting, ask someone to take detailed notes for you, including a verbatim record of key quotes and sound bites. If you can gain agreement from the participants, consider using a video or tape recorder, but be very sensitive to the impact of this on the conversation.*

4   Revisit the objectives and deliverables of the project

This is the point at which you ask 'what did we set out to do?' and 'what did we really achieve?'

Get clear about the original objectives

The facilitator may want to ask the customer or sponsor 'did you get what you wanted?'

It is then valuable to ask if the deadlines were met, and the satisfaction measures achieved.

Facilitator's notes:

- *Try and find the original 'criteria for success' to check whether the project delivered these.*

- *You can ask for original definitions of timescale, cost and resourcing.*

5   Go through the project step-by-step

In long or complex projects, it can be beneficial to revisit the project plan, compare it with what actually happened, and identify any deviation from the plan.

Create the 'big picture' if possible. Some teams chose to construct a flowchart of what happened, identifying tasks, deliverables and decision points. In this way, they can identify those parts of the project that experienced delays or were completed ahead of time, those parts that were particularly efficient or inefficient, and those parts where the team were unclear over what really happened.

OK. If you've got this far, then the context has been set for a powerful meeting. Silently congratulate yourself before moving on to the next section – this is where the fun starts!

6   Ask 'what went well?'

Start with what the participants feel good about Always start with the good points! We should be seeking to build on good practice as much as we are seeking to avoid repeat mistakes, recognizing and building on existing strengths. Ask 'What went really well in the project? What were the successful steps towards achieving your objective?'

Ask a 'why?' question several times. This will get you to the underlying reason.

> 'Our greatest success was hitting that first deadline.'

> *'Why was it that you were able to hit the deadline?'*

> 'We achieved the deadline mainly because we managed to get Jo and Emma working on the design at the last minute.'

> *'Why Jo and Emma?'*
>
> Why?

> 'Well, we had two other pressing projects, but Jo and Emma are a great team, and Jo had worked with BP before so she was able to rework some previous ideas.'

> *'Why were these ideas relevant this time?'*

> *'We've learned that BP always likes things done in a certain way - we know what works and what doesn't, and we know the design guidelines very well.'*

In this example from an Internet site design project, the use of repeated 'why' questioning has developed the success factor from being the ability to meet deadlines into the details of the historical working relationship and availability of guidelines.

Facilitator's notes:

- *Go around the room asking each individual for their successes. Don't let the loud ones dominate the meeting - it is vital that everyone is asked, and heard. Ask the quieter members for their ideas first, to prevent them hiding behind 'I was going to say that too'. The chances are that these insights will be less widely known by the others in the group than the opinions of the more vociferous staff. You may need to give them two minutes thinking time before anyone speaks, to write*

Ensure that all team members participate, involve the quiet ones early.

down what their successes were without being influenced by what others might say. It's OK if people choose the same example. Let each tell it in his or her own words.

- *If time is short, a technique that works is to say 'Give me your greatest success factor, the one that made the biggest difference. If someone has already covered it, choose your second greatest.'*

7 Find out why these aspects went well, and express the learning as advice for the future

Deal with experience rather than opinions. Feelings need to be acknowledged, but future recommendations have to be based on experience.

Press for specific, repeatable advice	Ask:

> *'What techniques or processes would be good to use again?'*

> *'How will we ensure future projects go just as well, or even better?'*

> *'What would your advice be to future project teams, based on your success here?'*

The main task here is to keep pressing for specific, repeatable advice.

Facilitator's notes:

- *This part of the meeting will be a conversation. You have two options. The first is to ask the probing questions (and let the conversation develop) as each person identifies their success factor(s). The idea is to reach group consensus advice through conversation. In a close team this will happen naturally.*

- *An alternative approach, useful if the team is more subdued, is to identify all the issues first, then choose the ones to work on as a team.*

Almost certainly, as discussion continues, 'bad' points as well as good will be discussed. Don't stifle this, let the discussion continue and encourage a positive phrasing of the advice. Asking for success factors is just a way to get the topics into the room, and should not be used to stifle discussion if the negatives creep in.

8 Then, ask 'what could have gone better?'

There are bound to be some areas where things could have gone better, where pitfalls were identified too late, and where process was sub-optimal. Ask 'what would enable you to deliver even more if you were starting again?'

> Even successes have room for improvement

Avoid letting people 'make others wrong' – rather, encourage them to say 'my view of the incident was different'. Remember that everyone's perception is equally valid.

This may be a time for personal disclosure. People often share things in this session that they have kept bottled up. During the chase to meet deadlines they haven't had the time to sit down together and be reflective. Frequently issues raised involve improved teamwork. Get people to focus on the activity or process rather than individuals.

Facilitator's notes:

- *Again, go round the room and ask each individual. It often makes sense to start with the team leader, who you have already asked to set the tone in being open. If he/she admits that 'things could have gone better', or more powerfully 'I could have done these things better', the rest of the team will open up too.*

Keep the focus on the future avoidance of past mistakes

Identify the stumbling blocks and pitfalls, so they can be avoided in future. The following questions are useful:

- 'Given what we knew at the time, what could we have done better?'

- 'Given the knowledge we have now, what can we do differently, in similar situations in future, to ensure success?'

- 'If you wanted to prevent a future project team from experiencing this difficulty, what would your advice be to them?'

- 'What would your advice be to future project teams based on your experiences here?'

Facilitator's notes:

- *Ensure that this section of the process does not become a witch-hunt or a finger-pointing exercise. It is OK to let people have their say, but rather than let them focus on the past ask 'So what would you do differently next time?'*

- *Consider writing on a flip chart: 'So what about next time?' to remind people of the focus of the meeting.*

- *Again you have the option to hold the discussion as each person identifies their points, or to collect the points and choose which to discuss.*

9　Ensure that the participants leave the meeting with their feelings acknowledged

You do not want anyone to leave the meeting feeling that key issues have not been aired, or that a valuable effort was not acknowledged. And you want people to have a sense of perspective between what went well and what they would do differently.

This can be achieved by asking people for a numerical rating of the project. Ask, 'looking back, how satisfied are you with this project; marks out of ten?' Many people will say 'the project was fine, no problems' and still give it eight out of ten. This enables you to ask 'what would have made it a ten for you?' and so access residual issues. Quite often some real gems come out at this stage. In one retrospect there was a real split in scores between the technical disciplines and the commercial and legal ones. The technical team rated the project at 8 out of 10 while the commercial view was a harsher 5. This created a whole new round of discussion as to why, something that had not come out in the earlier sharing.

> Use 'marks out of ten' to find out what is missing

During another one the team reflected on the impact of the process on the result – they acknowledged that it is still possible to still achieve a great outcome via an imperfect process.

Facilitator's notes:

- *It is worth giving them a few seconds thinking time and to write down their score before asking them to call it out, so they are not influenced by other people's ratings.*

- *If there was dissatisfaction in the room – perhaps someone felt a lack of acknowledgment – there may be steps that can be taken to address this even at this late stage in a project.*

10 Record the meeting

It is vital to have an interesting and well-structured account of the meeting and its outcomes. A suggested framework is:

- guidelines for the future, acting as hyperlinks to the rest of the document;

- history from the project to illustrate the guidelines;

- names of the people involved, a photograph of the group for future reference; and

- any key artefacts (e.g. documents, project plans).

This determines what you need to record from the meeting. Go to Chapter 12 to learn more about capturing knowledge.

Quotes bring the written account to life

The direct use of quotes is one of the most powerful ways of capturing the depth of feeling – and of creating a summary that is likely to be read.

'Nothing turns me off more than a ten-page report full of abstracted motherhood statements – I can already feel my eyes beginning to close ...'

Chris Collison

You see? Sprinkle selected quotes liberally throughout the write-up. Quotes are attributed to a person wherever possible. It goes without saying that the person attributed with any quote will need to agree to its inclusion.

A good way to summarize the lessons learned is as advice

Also record as accurately as possible what the advice or recommendations are for the future. Often recommendations won't be clearly stated in the meeting, and the facilitator may need to reframe the advice so it is generic. Express the advice as clearly, measurably and unambiguously as possible.

The acid test of the document's usefulness is to ask yourself, 'if I was the next project leader, would these lessons be any use to me?'

Ensure that you circulate the write-up around the participants for comment. Make sure nobody was misquoted, and that the facilitator's wording of the lessons really reflects the views of the team. Once agreed, distribute the final copy to the team. Consider also who else can benefit from the content and send it to them. Make it available as the basis for something even more powerful ...

What if a project was just starting up in three years time – how would they be prompted to read your record of events? The final stage is to find somewhere logical to store this invaluable document – somewhere where it will get read in detail and applied to future projects. Somewhere a group of people will review it and treat it as an asset to be embedded into future company processes and guidelines.

One way this has been refined is to capture people talking on video. For example when the political climate and BP's business priorities changed in the Middle East a project was 'mothballed' i.e. put on hold. The project team comprising BP staff and contract staff was being stood down. The political instability meant that it wasn't the first time that this had happened. The previous time, the team realized that there was a lot of re-learning to do, not just on technical matters but also relationships, cultural issues and logistical ones too, and they were determined for it not to happen again. The chances were when the project was again resurrected the team members would be involved in other projects or working for different companies and so they had to assume a new team would pick it up.

First a group of people from other projects were asked what they would most want to know if they were a newly formed team picking this up. They came up with a good list. A five minute overview, a 30 minute PowerPoint presentation, 'what to do in the first 30 days', who to go and talk to about key issues, the cultural obstacles, and then the technical detail for each discipline. This helped structure the process and knowledge into three levels of detail.

> Hearing others' perspectives on video

Each member of the team was then interviewed for an hour on video to capture their individual stories. The hours of interview were synthesized and 90-second sound bites were regrouped to illustrate the key themes, with links to the whole interview and to important documents. This was all saved onto a DVD. The draft was shown to the team to check for accuracy but it soon became apparent they wanted to watch more than their own contribution! It gave them a chance to hear the perspectives of other team members in a way they hadn't found time for in a face-to-face meeting.

They then held a face-to-face retrospect meeting for most of a day. It was a powerful meeting. The content on the video had raised awareness of some difficult issues, these were discussed openly and ideas for improving the project in future agreed. Because each issue was illuminated from several different perspectives it led to a greater understanding of the issue. Material from the retrospect was videoed and added to the final version. What the team realized was that some of the points for their own project were equally relevant to projects they were moving to. The principles for improvement were transferable.

Here's how an aid organization used the process to systematically learn from people's visits overseas.

Travellers tales

Tearfund is a UK-based relief and development agency, working in partnership with Christian agencies and churches around the world to tackle the causes and effects of poverty. They employ around 900 staff - one third in the UK or on short and long-term international placements, the remaining two thirds as national staff overseas.

In 2003, they introduced a new learning process into their organization to capture stories from employees returning from support and reconnaissance trips abroad. Based on a similar framework to the retrospect process, the learning tool was entitled 'Traveller Tales', and was designed to capture the human aspects of a visit through a 'one hour structured interview over a cappuccino', within a few days of their return.

Use questions to tease out stories

Rather than focus on generic learning points, the questions were deliberately designed to tease out stories:

> 'We have learned the importance of storytelling, particularly in an organization like Tearfund where profit is not the driving factor for managing knowledge and sharing learning. The most effective way to liberate these stories is by making interviews short, structured and fun.'
>
> Astrid Foxen, Knowledge Manager, Tearfund

The structured interview consisted of the following questions:

- Who was the most interesting person you met?

- What impressed you most on the visit?

- What struck you as novel on the trip?

- Did you come back with a story that you will be using when speaking about Tearfund in churches?

- What was the purpose of your visit and what did you learn?

- Practicalities:
  - visa,
  - accommodation,
  - money changing,
  - health tips,
  - security,
  - partner contact who organized the itinerary,
  - any other helpful people?

So how does this interview fit with other parts of Tearfund's knowledge management strategy?

When tickets are issued for travel overseas the travel administrator selects a person from a register of interviewers and informs them of the name of the person travelling and their return date. The interviewer then arranges to have coffee with the returning traveller during the first week after their return to undertake a structured interview.

Prior to travel, an email is also sent to the traveller reminding them of the 'Travel Tales folder', encouraging them to check to see if there is any useful information to help with planning their trip.

Following the interview the notes are written up, reviewed by the traveller and then made available electronically to the rest of the organization. And so the cycle continues.

As Astrid says:

> *'People are willing to participate as long as they perceive that they and their colleagues will benefit.'*

Meanwhile, in the commercial business of making money from diamonds, retrospect was also being applied.

Offshore diamond mining

De Beers is the world's leading diamond mining company; producing nearly 50 percent of the world's diamond supply by value. The De Beers operational base is in southern Africa, with major diamond production in South Africa, Namibia and Botswana. Although most of these mines are on land there are also considerable diamond-bearing deposits offshore Namibia, and on the northwest coast of South Africa.

De Beers began an involvement in knowledge management and intellectual capital in 2002, and Ian Corbett was chosen to head the project. Ian did some extensive research, and came to the conclusion that the BP approach to knowledge management (as described in this book) was probably the approach which would be most applicable to his own company. However, before committing to the BP knowledge management system, he wanted to pilot some of the components within De Beers, to make sure that they would work in a different organizational structure. His secondary objective for the pilots was to acquire material within De Beers for demonstrating the potential benefit of knowledge management to executives and senior leaders. Ian started looking around for a project which he could review using the retrospect process, and decided to select !Gariep.

The !Gariep project was a research and development project within De Beers Marine (the group that was exploring for offshore diamond-bearing deposits). It was an ambitious (high risk, high reward) project aimed at revolutionizing offshore mining technology, which ultimately failed to deliver. Despite the best efforts of everyone involved, the system which was dependent on a leap of faith, proved to be just too much of a stretch. The company had learned valuable lessons, but needed a way to capture, share and ultimately build on those lessons despite the disappointment with the project results.

Ian decided to employ the retrospect approach. He called in Nick Milton, of Knoco Ltd, and together they began to plan the sessions. Because the !Gariep project had lasted many years, spanned many work activities and involved many people, it was decided to split the project into four components, and retrospect each one separately. These components were:

> Split big projects into components and review separately

1   system design;

2   system construction;

3   system testing; and

4   system operation.

Each of these project components formed the focus for a half-day retrospect, where up to 12 carefully selected members of the project team sat around a hotel conference table and discussed exactly what happened on the project, what the success points were, and what they would have done differently with the benefit of hindsight. As one of the participants said afterwards:

> '*I found the process very engaging. It wasn't easy to drift away; I found the content riveting - it kept you engaged. It was a lot of asking very obvious questions, but for those who were attached deep into the project, perhaps the questions weren't quite as obvious, and lifting that out is the fine art. There was an elegant simplicity about it, the questions weren't complex. They were very open-ended, and people did latch onto them and open up quite nicely.*
>
> *The benefits to the company as a whole will be tremendous, and at the personal level too it is a huge developmental step. And, of course, the reductions in the learning curve for those who follow on.*'

The retrospect was seen as a great success by those who took part, and when Ian presented the output to senior managers, they also were convinced about the suitability of the process to help improve performance through learning. In particular, they were impressed by video output of a young engineer talking passionately and eloquently about the lessons, and about how the company could do better next time!

In fact the company DID do better next time! Nearly two years later, Nick Milton held a retrospect for the !Gariep Phase 2 project (which had involved a major and innovative ship conversion in Newcastle). !Gariep Phase 2 was seen as a massive success. Having learned lessons from !Gariep Phase 1 and other projects, the team were able to bring !Gariep Phase 2 to success-ful completion several months ahead of schedule. This success flowed from clearly identifying and understanding the value of detailed upfront planning, a theme highlighted in the output of the !Gariep retrospect.

The level of attention paid to the selection and integration of a number of partners to execute the latest !Gariep conversion proved to be a critical success factor, as it enabled the value and benefit of detailed upfront planning to reach new levels at De Beers Marine. Extensive knowledge-sharing due to the excellent relationship developed with the key partners underpinned the success. Their expertise and experience introduced substantial new knowledge and capability into the project team, which enabled the technical limit for such a major conversion to be challenged through further refinement of the detailed planning and scheduling. The innovative solution would not otherwise have been possible, which demonstrates the criticality of forging networks with the right people to release value!

The *!Gariep* is now actively mining diamonds offshore Namibia.

Nick Milton, Ian Corbett

Here are some lessons from applying the retrospect process in different settings:

1   Get the environment right for the meeting, something that brings back the memories.

2   Keep asking *'Why?'* to get to the root cause.

3   Have a customer for the knowledge gleaned, in the room if possible.

4   Express what you have learned as guidelines or advice for others.

5   Give everyone a chance to share their experience and per-
     ceptions.

6   Use quotes and/or video-clips to bring the capture to life.

The last three chapters have discussed ways of sharing knowledge - by learning before, during and after. But how do we find
the right people with the right knowledge at the right time?

Everything that we have discussed in the book so far depends heavily on people connecting with people. But how do you ensure that the *right* people connect?

In this chapter:

- The importance of managing know-who, and stimulating connections between people.

- Why personal homepages are a powerful foundation for knowledge sharing.

- How to create and introduce a successful knowledge directory.

Unnatural actions

Louise teaches six-year-olds in a primary school in West London – close to Heathrow Airport. Each morning, just before starting their work, the class participates in an activity known as 'brain gym'. All of the children perform 'unnatural actions' such as folding their arms, then folding them in a counter-intuitive way. If you are right-handed, you will naturally place your right forearm over your left – try left over right. Other activities involve 'simultaneously patting your head and rubbing your chest', and reciting the alphabet whilst moving alternate arms and legs. It's a hilarious sight at times, but brain gym is more than a humorous ice-breaker.

Creating the connections that improve learning performance

Accelerated learning theory suggests that such actions stimulate the left and right-hand side of the brain simultaneously, creating neural connections across the *corpus callosum*. The end result of this increased neural activity is that each child is *more receptive to learning*.

What has accelerated learning theory got to do with knowledge management?

If you consider teams, divisions, business units or even newly-merged companies, there is a tendency for knowledge to align itself with organizational constructs. When this is the case, learning is likely to occur in parallel – in ignorance of what another part of the organization is doing.

> Think about when you first came to work for your current organization. How long did it take you to develop the relationships, contacts and networks that you now have? You might even want to draw a map of these.
>
> Now imagine what you could have achieved if you had been able to make these connections in a fraction of the time.

At the time of their merger, BP and Amoco were like the left and right-hand sides of the brain. The immediate integration challenge was the creation of an environment where relationships were forced beyond their natural boundaries – stimulating the breakdown and re-creation of networks and communities, and encouraging staff to think beyond their normal circles of influence. In this way, learning could occur by the connections between both sides of the brain, or organization.

Creating the environment to enable connections

So how do you create such an environment? An environment that puts you in touch with people who *know*?

Making connections requires more than the mechanical bringing together of the right people. Unlike neurons in the brain, people exhibit more complex behaviour! A desire to learn and the willingness to share are two of the factors which need to be present for a truly effective connection to occur.

BP took a bottom-up approach, to develop a knowledge directory that gained the buy-in of many thousands of staff. The product was known as 'Connect'.

Connect took the form of a searchable intranet repository, through which all staff could search for people with relevant knowledge and experience. Additionally, they could easily create a personal homepage rich in content, which in turn would be accessible to anyone with network access.

Learning before doing

Investing some time learning before from other corporate, yellow-pages initiatives proved to be time well spent for Connect. We held a peer assist (see Chapter 7, Learning from your Peers) with staff at Microsoft, Glaxo Wellcome, Hughes Space and Communications and Proctor & Gamble, which yielded the following findings:

Three key lessons from the experiences of others

- keep the vision clear;

- manage the relationship with the HR department; and

- ensure that ownership lies with individuals.

Let's look at these in a little more detail.

Keep the vision clear

Clear vision. What is the underlying vision of what we are trying to achieve here? What is distinctive about a corporate yellow pages, relative to other directories or resource planning systems?

In BP's case, they were striving for an environment where all employees could easily search for people with the relevant expertise, and they could all create and maintain a personal homepage on the intranet.

Then would follow a series of conversations between the searcher and the resulting staff – perhaps little more than a ten-minute telephone call. Enough of a conversation to prevent a wheel being re-invented, just enough to share a successful insight or a nugget of key commercial intelligence.

> Generating ten-minute telephone calls is where the value lies

When we talk about resource management, we sometimes think in terms of allocating people into roles, as though they can only make a contribution if we change their place in the organization – if they sit in a different seat. The *real* resource to manage is the knowledge and experience that resides in the heads of your employees – regardless of where their backside is at the time!

The transfer of knowledge is all about people and relationships rather than projects and resources – hence an environment to support knowledge management needs to respect people as people, present them as people, and provide ways for them to key into relationships with others.

Complementing, not competing with HR systems

This is not the traditional realm of HR information systems, which exist for a different purpose. The information in such systems tends to be owned by the HR department.

For such a *knowledge management* system to be successful, BP's experience was that ownership needs to reside with the individuals concerned. This is their personal, alternative prospectus – how they want to be known, rather than how the company knows them. As such, it complements existing people systems rather than replaces them. It helps build a living, breathing, three-dimensional representation of a person – far broader than a set of work histories or training records.

Creating an employee-owned knowledge directory is a laudable aim and one which others will be quick to exploit. Expect to be approached by people with their own agendas who will be keen to 'enhance' your environment beyond all recognition through a series of minor additions – pick your allies and negotiating strategy carefully!

Perhaps you're thinking 'That's all very well for large organizations, but what about my company of 50, or even 500 staff – do I really need such a system?'

For 50 people, you probably don't. You probably know everyone in the company fairly well. But do you know them well enough to know what they need? You might consider a simple

> Knowledge directories in small companies

approach – even paper-based – where staff can post their offers of assistance and requests for help (see the 'Who's Who in Marketing' example from Centrica later in this chapter). This may reveal some unexpectedly hidden talents, and liberate a new, informal marketplace for knowledge. Additionally you may network with people in other organizations. Do you know who you need to know to do your job?

For 500 people, especially where they are split across more than one office, some form of system will be a valuable resource. Something that simply lists what people know about and what help they need, linked to their contact details, could make a big difference. The authors are aware of several small companies who rely on systems similar to Connect in their sophistication.

The value of personal information

A consultant colleague often quotes the phrase:

> *'There's no such thing as strictly business – everything is personal.'*
>
> Brad Meyer

Business relationships flourish when personal details are shared.

Isn't this the reason why golf clubs flourish? Isn't it the basis on which salespeople operate?

If this maxim holds true, then the ramifications for the content of any knowledge directories are significant. Remember, our vision is to generate ten-minute conversations that act as the catalysts for effective knowledge exchange. Think back to the last time you had a ten-minute conversation with someone. Perhaps it was on a flight or at a conference? What are the sorts of things you might cover during that ten minutes?

- Where do you work?

- What is your job?

Work-related information is only the tip of the iceberg

OK, fairly mundane so far. So, we continue looking for common ground:

- Do you know James, I think he used to work in your head office?

- Did you go to that conference in St. Andrews?

- Do you play golf?

- What's your handicap?

- What about your partner, does he/she play too?

- Do you have children? How many of each?

Let's stop here and look at what's happening. We're spiralling out from the conventional work-related areas, and looking to connect at deeper levels – through shared experiences, social similarities and emotional challenges.

Now, go back ten minutes and imagine that you already knew the answers to those questions. How much easier is it now to establish rapport, trust and a working relationship with this person?

Now imagine that you had instant access to this level of knowledge about everyone in your organization. That's powerful. And that's why creating space for people to express the less formal side of their lives is so important to any knowledge directory.

It's almost as if you can know a person before you meet or speak with them.

> The power of knowing people before meeting them

People's Connect pages could contain an enormous variety of 'soft' information. The following three excerpts illustrate this:

> *'I have two great kids that I like spending time with while they still like spending it with me. We are very involved in our Church. I enjoy hunting and fishing with my 13-year-old son. He enjoys fishing, so we fish. We went for five days, way out in the wilderness, on a float-fishing trip in Alaska last summer. I enjoy supervising a good team of engineers and I like having a great time doing so. I like delivering big projects like Schiehallion when I was the Wells Team Leader there.'*
> *'I think it's a good idea to continue through life learning new*

skills, although I think both my piano teacher and Spanish teacher wish I'd give up trying!'

'I'm married with a three-year-old daughter, Martha, who occupies most of my free time, and we have another on the way! I live 3 miles from Sunbury, in Shepperton – pretty close to the Red Lion Pub and the river! If you're turned on by personality profiling, I'm: ENFP (Myers Briggs), Plant/Resource Investigator (Belbin), Creator Innovator (TMI).'

Sometimes it only takes a small amount of disclosure to spark a conversation, and low-technology solutions can go a surprisingly long way to get things moving.

Centrica's *Who's Who in Marketing*

Centrica is a large organization consisting of a number of customer-facing brand units (including British Gas, One.Tel and Direct Energy). These brand units are in turn supported by a marketing community of several hundred staff across the group. In late 2003, cross-brand working and communication across that community was felt to be sub-optimal – the organization wasn't living up to it's aim to be 'greater than the sum of its parts'. Digging a little deeper into the reasons for this, it was established that, rather than a reluctance to work together, the primary reason for insular behaviour was simply that people didn't know who to talk to, work with, or ask for help. The relationships simply didn't exist, and the habits hadn't been formed.

As a rapid, low-cost response to this, the leadership team sponsored an initiative to create a physical *Who's Who in Marketing* book, organized by the activities that they perform on a day-to-day basis or the skills and expertise that they possess.

Who's Who in Marketing took the form of an A5-sized address book. Whilst online solutions have built-in maintainability, the marketing managers across Centrica expressed a preference for a physical book as a first step.

The key objective for the 'Who's Who' is to give people access to new contacts without them first knowing a name. Entry into the directory was entirely voluntary. Information was collected via e-mail, and then organized by areas of marketing activity. People were then listed according to whether their day-to-day tasks or their expertise fell within that area. Importantly, a little informal personal information was also included just to give an insight into the person you might be contacting, or to act as an ice-breaker. The question to prompt this was 'What makes you happy?'

Find a prompt for personal information

Responses to this section were varied and revealing!

- Barbeques and cold beer when somebody else is cooking ...

- Sunshine and Saturday mornings

- Working with people you can trust and rely on

- Chilling with a cold margarita, boarding on a lake

- Creativity, being on the cutting edge of new technology

- Skiing in Vermont, hot apple cider and a roaring log fire

- My children (especially when asleep!)

- Being in the mountains

- Freedom to explore and develop new ideas

- Chocolate (and lots of it!)

Feedback from the marketing community was very positive:

- *'Well put together piece with the nice little touch of something personal about each of the people - two thumbs up!'*

- *'The "What makes me happy" section provides some useful insight into colleagues you know well/may meet in the future – it can be a useful talking point.'*

The marketing community learned that a physical directory is instantly accessible, and available long after their computers have been switched off. Furthermore it is a highly cost-effective mechanism for reaching isolated members of a community in organizations where there is an incomplete IT infrastructure. Inevitably there are issues of keeping the information current and concerns about the sensitivity of the information in the wrong hands.

Informality and personal disclosure makes the difference – providing sufficient intrigue for most participants to look up their colleagues, and discover the secrets of their satisfaction! The 'What makes me happy' section became a valuable strapline for the initiative.

The ingredients of a typical 'Connect' homepage

BP's 'Connect' was a more ambitious online environment – let's take a look at what made up a typical 'homepage'.

- Name (the name you are known by – not necessarily the one your mother, or the Payroll system, uses!)

- Job title

- Team business unit

- Free text area

- Structured taxonomy of 'areas of expertise'

- Languages spoken

- Internal and external contacts

- Favourite Web links (internal and external)

- Uploaded photograph

- Uploaded *résumé* (CV)

- Uploaded audio clip

- Membership of networks and communities of practice

- Basic contact information – including telephone numbers, e-mail addresses etc.

The process for creating these detail-rich pages was supported by templates, *very* simple templates! Nobody needed to write HTML, or even know what it stood for – just the ability to think, type and click, and most importantly of all, the willingness to be contacted.

I don't know what to write!

This is a common complaint for a variety of reasons. For some, natural modesty is the barrier. Others find it hard to précis appropriately. A commonly observed phenomenon is 'writer's block false start'.

With the best of intentions, the author starts with a sentence or two, stalls, and then becomes distracted. Faced with the prospect of leaving a part-finished page, the author falls victim to a self-imposed culture of perfection, and deletes what he or she has already written, under the self-conscious misapprehension that it is better to say nothing, than to say something incomplete.

> Freeform text is valuable and needs to be encouraged by the right questions

In order to make it easy for people, Connect prompted the writer with the following open questions.

- What are you currently working on?

- What areas have you worked on in the past?

- What subjects might you like to be contacted about?

- What do you enjoy doing?

- Is there any help that you need?

Some staff worked through these questions in a structured manner, whilst others used them as prompts for ideas. In either case, the resultant page had thoughtful content, owned by the individual.

Voluntary and non-validated – a truly employee-owned approach

In fact, *only* the individuals concerned could update their pages – not their line managers, team secretaries or the HR department – just the individuals themselves. The content was non-validated – it was assumed that staff would be honest in the information they provided.

During the credibility-building stages of the project, professional coaches were employed to floor-walk and help staff through the process of constructing their page, including the freeform areas. Whilst effective in securing high quality content, BP was unable to scale-up the approach satisfactorily. However, the good examples created during this phase serves as 'seeds' for others struggling for inspiration.

Direct support, coaching and peer-review can produce high quality content

When 200 staff in British Gas's Finance function embarked on their own mini 'Connect' project, they used an internal conference to launch the initiative, taking 30 minutes there and then to write the first draft of their pages. They then buddied-up with three others to review each others' pages. Asking the question *'Does this sound like me?'* of a colleague can be a useful process for stimulating the most helpful content.

A picture is worth a thousand words

About a third of BP staff provided a picture of themselves. Many of these were your regular head-and-shoulders, passport-style shots – very useful for identification, but not as informative as they could have been.

> Informal photographs create a three-dimensional picture of the person. Head-and-shoulders shots are for passports!

By far the more interesting images were the more personal, human-interest shots. Family groups, staff standing proudly beside their treasured cabriolet, private plane, caravan(!), or even vintage motorcycle. Action shots of people skiing, image-enhanced morphing animations, Disney cartoons, baby pictures, pet-poses, even the odd glamour shot – albeit well within the bounds of absolute decency – were just some examples.

The award for 'most innovative photo' went to Dave, who embedded real-time shots of himself working at his desk via a static camera. Not only could you read all about Dave's detailed experience, background and hobbies – you can assess whether now is a good time to call him by the expression on his face, or the current level of his coffee cup.

Some day soon all this will be mundane, but for now, 'Dave-cam' remains a great source of amusement for those who happen upon it unsuspectingly.

The structure–freedom equation

Provide for different working styles – structure and freedom both have their place in a knowledge directory

Different people are comfortable working with different levels of structure. Some find it constraining, some find it liberating. Many people would blanch at the prospect of filling a blank sheet of paper with a story about themselves. Some would rebel at the prospect of ticking the boxes that relate to them.

The common-sense solution then, is to provide an environment which caters for both preferences – life's box-tickers as well as life's lyricists.

The technological implications of this are significant. The power of any search technology is reliant on a common way of describing the same concept – a common language or taxonomy. By equipping the user community with a detailed pick-list of terms, an implicit common language is created.

> 'Give me the names and faces of all the Chicago-based French-speakers with expertise in negotiating and e-commerce.'

Easy enough. Relational databases have had this capability for years. However, to rely exclusively on structured 'database' searches presupposes that all potential requirements can be captured within a simple taxonomy.

'Find me everyone who has any relationship with Chevron.'
'Find me people with a passion for fly fishing.'

These ad-hoc queries require more general free-text searches. Again, providing for both requirements is the best way to engage a broad base of staff in to using a knowledge directory.

The creation and roll-out of BP's 'Connect'

Connect was an opportunity always waiting to happen, but one which required a degree of coordination. Prior to its first incarnation in late 1997, there were no less than twelve independent 'Who's Who' directories at BP. Each one served its own community and there was no collective effort to align or integrate these islands of information, or even transfer the requirements, or lessons learned, from one system to the next.

When a thirteenth directory showed signs of appearing, it was time to find a more intelligent way of tackling this business need. A workshop was arranged, and for the first time, a specification was created for a system that had the potential to satisfy the needs of the entire organization.

> Buy-in from the top of the organization is well worth persevering for

Gaining buy-in from some of the most senior staff sent a powerful signal to the organization. Naturally, Lord Browne was already known to every employee. However, the fact that he agreed to have a homepage with photograph, career history and some informal information about his hobbies and interests sent a strong message to the company that he implicitly supported the initiative. Even if you have to prepare a printed example in advance in order to ease the way with the support staff that typically surround senior executives, the payback is worthwhile. Negotiate tenaciously!

A prototype was created, based around the requirements of a pilot community of 500 technical staff – staff whose leadership had generously agreed to invest in a tool that had the

Bring together the potential and existing stakeholders and engage them in the design of the future

potential to serve the entire organization. This pilot phase was used to test the principles and technology. Changes were fed back into the design throughout this time, and additional small focus groups were used to broaden the design critique. Within six months the number of people with Connect homepages had grown to over 1000. At this point, with a credible set of early adopters, a concerted internal marketing campaign was initiated.

Persuading several thousand staff to each spend 15 minutes creating a personal homepage is a non-trivial exercise. Given the underlying philosophy that this was to be a non-mandatory, bottom-up initiative, the most effective way of delivering Connect as a company-wide environment was to deliver through others.

Connect 'champions' were informally recruited as part of the underground campaign – these were staff from any background who believed in its potential, and were willing to give a few hours of their time to promote it within their own business unit or network.

Make use of local volunteers, and their innovative ideas wherever possible

Thirty staff volunteered to run local marketing initiatives – ranging from traditional presentations, 'donut talks' and exhibition stands with digital cameras and scanners, through to competitions between teams, with champagne for the first team to be 'fully connected', and some highly innovative local approaches. In Alaska, the two-litre milk cartons that graced the staff restaurant were embellished with 'wanted posters' that carried the photograph of a local employee, with a few words describing their background or experience. The implicit challenge to the breakfasters was to go back to their desks and use Connect to identify the face that they had been staring at over their cornflakes.

Make use of tokens for recognition, however trivial the value

A thousand 'Connect pens' were purchased, and used to great effect as token recognition from the project leader for staff who set good examples. An encouraging and grateful e-mail was sent to such a page owner, notifying them that a pen was on its way to them. The e-mail finished with a request to tell other staff in their areas about Connect, and yielded great rewards – up to a hundredfold. Many Connect champions were drawn in through this simple process – all from the investment of a $5 pen!

Regardless of the culture, stories are a consistently powerful way to augment a marketing campaign, and using anecdotes to illustrate the power of a tool like Connect has been highly successful.

Consider the following example, taken from a note from a marketing manager in Tanzania to a Connect champion in Singapore.

From: Mondoloka, Fumu

Sent: 07 July 1998 15:18

To: Abrahams, Andrea D (Singapore)

Subject: RE: Does it work?

> **Success stories are the most powerful marketing material**

Andrea,
Connect is a brilliant tool!
To walk you through the highlights of the breweries story:
I had a calling to innovate an offer for Tanzania Breweries which is under South African Breweries and we do not exactly have all the SAB accounts in the region. BP (Tanzania) put in a bid and are tipped to be awarded but we have to get the business and lock it up.
I searched on Connect for Sector expertise pulled a few names and sent an e-mail detailing my request. To my amazement the spiral of help the process yielded was incredible. We got from the network a blueprint of an offer made to a Scottish Brewery which we might not implement in its form but is a sound basis for us to kit one together.

> My colleagues from Tanzania & I are currently assessing
> what we can draw from it & I should travel to Dar es
> Salaam in two weeks to gather with the guys there the
> information we need then we'll zero in on the offer.
> No proof of the pudding yet but we shall certainly share
> it with every one that helped when the deal is done,
> which I am sure is going to be soon.
> Fumu

Incidentally, the deal *did* get done.

This story could be read online as part of Connect, together with ten others. Having a distributed network of local champions made it relatively easy to get a flow of examples and stories to pass on to others, and to write-up for internal magazines and presentations.

In each case, Connect was promoted as fun, alternative and individual. And it worked!

E-mail jokes have a capacity to spread, virus-like, across an organization. During the summer of 1998, someone, somewhere in BP decided to create the following e-mail signature:

I'm connected: *http://connect.bpWeb.bp.com/searchid=82025*
Are you? *http://connect.bpWeb.bp.com*

E-mail signature files have virus-like capacity to spread – make use of them!

Within a few months, the signature file had been copied and customized by thousands of staff.

Knowing where to start

Find a starting place in the organization that will yield quick wins

Choosing the right pilot community is critical to the early success of a knowledge directory, so where is the most fertile soil to begin sowing the seeds?

In piloting and launching Connect, BP found four different indicators that were consistent with rapid uptake.

- *Staff who have clear internal customers.* This included internal consultants, HR and IT professionals, shared service groups and technologists. Anybody who has a need to be visible to a constituency is likely to view tools like Connect as a positive vehicle for their own agenda.

- *Staff who work in geographically dispersed teams, networks and communities.* Because of the global nature of BP's business, many teams work across several locations. More significantly, networks and communities of practice have strong roles to play in sharing know-how, but meet very infrequently. In both cases, through learning more about a remote colleague's background, seeing their picture and understanding more about their immediate environment, relationships are strengthened. With the right level of coordination, tools like Connect can be used as effective distributed ice-breakers.

- *Businesses which are geographically remote.* BP operates in over 100 countries worldwide, including some inhospitable environments. At times, the distance could lead frontier teams into attempted self-sufficiency, sub-optimal performance and personal frustration. Positioning a tool like Connect as a way of remaining attached to the body of the company and tapping into the resources of tens of thousands of staff is easy with such groups, and the quid pro quo of individuals making themselves available as well as asking for help, followed quickly.

- *Businesses or departments with new leadership.* When leadership is renewed, the relationship-building process usually needs to start all over again. Some leaders saw Connect as an ideal way for them to visualize and begin to informally 'know' their staff. Others made a habit of bringing up someone's Connect page on the screen whilst talking to them on the telephone in order to have more effective conversations.

Embedding into business processes

The final part of the marketing strategy was to target some of the core people-processes for the company. Staff joining and leaving, and staff development training in particular.

As part of the induction process, new recruits in BP are introduced to Connect and encouraged to use it to extend their networks and introduce themselves to others.

Business processes can be used as powerful prompts

Conversely, when leaving the company, staff were entitled to delegate ownership of their page to a colleague who was remaining inside BP, as a fragment of corporate memory and as a potential calling card.

Finally, staff attending some leadership development courses and internal conferences were encouraged to find out about their fellow attendees through their entries in Connect. These reminders served to institutionalize the usage of Connect, and spread the word.

Providing valuable context by linking information with its owner

In addition to answering the 'Who knows about...?' questions, a Web-based collection of personal homepages has a large secondary benefit.

Link information to the people who know

Because every individual entry in Connect had a unique URL, each page could then be linked to, from other Web pages and applications.

This was a powerful benefit as it enabled Web content to be linked to individuals in a context-rich way. Traditionally, Web pages might contain a 'mailto:' link at the foot of each page linking the content to an owner.

Why do people search the Web – intranet, extranet, Internet for information? What do *you* expect as a return on your invested time, beyond the sheer entertainment of searching and finding?

- For some people the expected outcome is hard information – 'give me something that I can print off and act upon with confidence'.

- For others, it will be a set of leads for further research – using the information landscape as a brainstorming environment.

- For the remainder it might be a set of contacts to pursue for further information, or to confirm the information that has already been provided.

Where the quality of the information can't always be guaranteed – often the case in large corporate intranets that have grown organically – the integrity of the owner contact information can be as valuable as the content itself.

> Intranets can be used as places to meet people, as well as find information

The content is essentially an advertisement for a conversation with the owner.

In these cases, being able to switch instantly from reading the *content* to reading about the *author*, through a single click of the mouse, is of tremendous value. This extra context increases the likelihood of a conversation taking place, and may improve the effectiveness of that conversation as a vehicle for knowledge transfer.

Here's an example.

> Personal homepages provide the context behind the information

Anne is searching the intranet for information relating to business in Azerbaijan. She discovers a page authored two years previously by Bob, and wonders whether the commercial climate has changed during the elapsed two years. She clicks on the e-mail link on the page and starts to write Bob a mail.

Half way through, she starts to feel a bit foolish – like a cold caller, and considers backing out, or taking the information at face value. However, she perseveres, completes and sends the note.

Since Bob moved location six months ago, and his e-mail address changed, Anne's attempt bounces, and the effort is wasted.

Here's another take on the same example.

Anne is searching the intranet for information relating to business in Azerbaijan. She discovers a page authored two years previously by Bob, and wonders whether the commercial climate has changed during the elapsed two years. She clicks on the link on the page that links to Bob's personal homepage, looks thoughtfully at his photograph and starts to read all about him.

Half way through, she discovers that like her, he has experience in integrated marketing and call centre management. Encouraged by this, she checks his contact details and telephones him, noting that he returned to Aberdeen earlier in the year.

Anne and Bob now have two children and live on the outskirts of Edinburgh.

OK, so the last bit is stretching the point a little! However, this example illustrates the power of relatedness between individuals and the value of photographs and autobiography to help generate this.

In BP today, seven years after its launch, thousands of intranet pages link to Connect pages – names in business unit organigrams, group photographs, page owner links all redirect to people's personal homepages.

All this sounds a little mundane, but it represents a significant shift in how people approach their information resources. BP's intranet became a place where you 'meet people' rather than just 'find information'. Context as well as content; know-who as well as know-how.

Details, and access to a demonstration of the Connect product used by BP and other organizations are available on the Learning to Fly CD included with this book.

Connecting the BBC

With 25,000 staff located the UK and spread around the world, the BBC understands the challenge of knowing 'who is who' and 'who has done what'. There are many functions which are shared across the organization but which are spread across regional sites (World Service, and the main production centres in London, Bristol, and the national centres for Scotland, Wales and Northern Ireland). Keeping in touch with other people who do the same job as you but for a different part of the BBC can be hard and there is a real risk of people 're-inventing the wheel' simply because they don't know what already exists. Euan Semple, Head of Knowledge Management picks up the story ...

'Three years ago, apart from the online version of the Corporate Directory, there were no tools to help staff network and collaborate. More and more staff were becoming aware of the power of the Internet to help identify like-minded individuals and connect with them but we weren't making it easy for them to do this at work. Indeed there were situations where craft staff were spending more time networking on the Internet with editors in the US than they were with editors in the next door cutting room.

'The first networking tool introduced was a Q&A tool that allowed any member of staff to ask a question which could then be read, and answered by any of the other 25,000 or so people in the corporation. The BBC took a deliberately low-

key approach to promoting the use of the tool, preferring word of mouth rather than high profile publicity as a way of encouraging trust and engagement in a tool which relies on openness and willingness to share. The results were amazing with 'talk.gateway' getting 90,000 visits each month and effectively answering a wide range of questions on every conceivable topic.

'What talk showed was that there was a population out there willing to use online tools and to do so in pursuit of real work issues and problem solving - next thing was to help them find out more about each other. We knew we wanted a tool which would enhance people's ability to find each other and gain greater insight into what knowledge existed in the organization.'

Euan contacted both Shell and BP as large, dispersed organizations already active in using online tools as a means of making and maintaining contact between staff. When talking with BP they became aware of Connect, its history and development.'

Develop a shopping list of needs

For the BBC, having completed their 'learning before doing', there were a number of key features already on their shopping list:

- Control of the information which is volunteered. All of these new online tools require a degree of disclosure which not everyone is comfortable with. It is essential that people feel that they can trust the use to which any information they expose is going to be put. The more they are in control of what gets shared, the better.

- The personal nature of the pages mattered. We wanted the pictures to be prominent and to encourage our staff to share more than just career information about themselves. Being able to express outside work interests, hobbies, external links and sources all adds to the rich picture you are able to build up about the person.

- The combination of structured and unstructured data was very important. We needed a product which integrated with our corporate directories, and allowed us to layer a taxonomy of interests and skills and to adapt this taxonomy to fit our own business easily. Being able to add to the list of topics and manage their organic growth was very important.

- The ability for staff to set up 'community pages' for their own interest groups – to manage their own networks through the system.

Since its successful introduction into the BBC, Euan has seen Connect used in a number of ways.

'The most popular use is as an address book. Looking up someone in Connect at the very least gets you their phone number etc. but if they have filled in their page then, as you are talking to them, you can find out a little bit about them, their background and interests, all of which adds to the richness of the conversations you can have with them and encourages social interaction and increased trust.

'The second most common use is as a means of identifying groups of like-minded individuals. These have been used to reveal those in the BBC who have skills as facilitator and provide a quick way of finding people willing to offer this service. It has also been used to identify people interested in particular areas of craft skill and to form the invite list to presentations relevant to that area of expertise. In the last example, Connect has been used to identify those in the business interested in strategic thinking about technology and has been a useful sounding board for new ideas.

'We are also building Connect into a wider programme of work establishing formal and informal communities within the BBC, and in the future we will integrate Connect with our Q&A tool so that users can easily move from online conversations to pages about the participants and relevant groups they are in.

'The highly networked environment we are creating allows individuals to connect, support each other and take action in ways never before experienced in organizations. Where the telephone and the telegraph were the communication tools that drove the expansion of the modern organization as we

currently understand it e-mail, the Web and tools like Connect will form part of entirely new ways of looking at organizations both in work and civic life. It is exciting to be part of it!'

Capitalizing on the existing knowledge of our employees

HBG is a Dutch-based contractor, recently merged with Royal BAM/NBM Group, with 20,000 employees operating in the fields of civil engineering, in the Netherlands, Germany, the US and the UK. Consultancy and contracting are performed worldwide. Jorden Hagenbeek, former knowledge management engineer at HBG summarized the challenge that HBG faced.

> *'Since our product was knowledge – we sell the knowledge to complete complex projects such as airports, ports and manu-facturing plants – we needed to capitalize on the existing knowledge of our employees.'*

HBG's knowledge management team decided to approach the company employees as 'clients' – an internal market.

'Our market research showed us that, from our clients' perspective, the main requirement for knowledge products should be *enjoyment*. Working with our products had to be fun, or a company-wide KM initiative would simply be another obligation. Our KM products had to be of outstanding quality; otherwise our market would surely reject it. This all meant that our project had become more challenging, but more fun, too!'

Jorden summarized his findings as:

> *'No one enjoys obligations. HBG's culture is professional and technocratic; people want to solve problems but don't like to be told to do so.*
>
> *'Externalizing knowledge is difficult. Employees learn a great deal while being on a project, but once the project has ended, it's hard to externalize the lessons learned in a way that becomes reusable for another project. People need to talk more!*

> '*Everyone enjoys a social gathering. HBG employees expressed their appreciation for professional events that foster socializing, where food and drink make for a more casual feeling among employees. People tend to find each other during these events and the research showed the relationships established during these sessions are durable.*'

It was clear to the team that a technical, database-oriented approach wouldn't work for knowledge management in HBG and that reports and intranets would not be successful either. HBG developed their own expertise-sharing tool to allow employees to access a database of each employee's skill-sets with minimal effort. The concept behind HBG Connect was to connect the knowledgeable employees within HBG via the company's intranet. Employees wouldn't have to write down all they knew, but rather just describe the highlights of their background and current projects in a homepage. This structure gives a searcher enough *information to decide whether to contact the knowledge-owner or not.*

The team articulated their strategy by framing everything for employees in a positive light:

1 *We enable you to participate* by creating the time and tools that will make your work easier to complete and more fun to do;

2 *We challenge you to participate* by making yourself known to the rest of the company. It's vital for the success of your work, your colleagues, and the company;

3 *We communicate successes*. Each time a result is achieved with knowledge management we use it as a marketing tool. Everybody likes to be a part of success.

So what are the lessons from these examples of creating a directory of people willing to share what they know?

1   Have a clear vision and stick to it, don't let it become a directory for all purposes.

2   Make it personal, have formal and informal parts, structured and unstructured, include photos, make it fun and easy to use.

3   Make it simple to complete and simple to update, let the individual want to keep her information current.

4   Consider starting with a physical book. This has advantages of ready access, but issues of updating and sensitivity.

5   Make the system self-sustaining. Embed it into people's processes and deeply integrate it into the company intranet. Connect to every site.

6   Start where the energy is and deliver the repository through local enthusiasts.

7   Let leaders and sponsors set a good example both by entering their information and searching for others.

8   Success stories encourage others to use it.

9   Include pages for communities to use to identify themselves.

10   Plan the next phase now, to change the way information is offered.

Whilst a tool like Connect enables the creation of a transient set of contacts, more permanent and formal networks play an equally important part in knowledge sharing. The next chapter explores the vital role of networks and communities of practice as both the guardians and channels of a company's knowledge.

Oh, and you can stop trying to pat your head and rub your stomach now!

Networking and Communities of Practice

In the last chapter we talked about how we stay connected with those who know in order to have a ten-minute conversation at the right time. What about staying connected with groups of people having a common interest or topic? In this chapter we will take a look at:

- Why people find the time to help others.

- The life cycle of a community and some definitions.

- Launching a community.

- Building momentum.

- Being part of the community.

- Sustaining a community.

- Closing communities.

- Networks as the stewards of the company's knowledge.

It was 3 February. Somewhere in the control room at a refinery in Australia John, a plant inspector, was planning the inspection schedule for the following week. He sent an e-mail

Networks ...

requesting some advice from his network about the inspection of fan blades and hubs on cooling fan units. By 11 a.m. the following morning Steve, an inspector at Salt Lake City Refinery, had responded with some reports of repeated hub failures; in 1985, 1989 and again in 1997. The gist of the report was that it was due to the U-bolts that hold the blades to the hub not being properly tightened. After holding discussions with the manufacturer, the procedure manual was amended to recommend installing a protective guard and performing preventative maintenance at 6-12 month intervals.

On 7 February a network member passed this advice on to a larger network in the exploration and production stream of the business. One member of this network passed it on to a further hundred people he felt ought to know. One of these sent it to his local team of twenty maintenance engineers and so on ...

... taking and applying the learning

John the inspector in Australia took heed of the recommendations, and he was not the only one. By 30 March, the Hemphill Gas plant in Texas, as a result of the warning, had inspected 16 fan units even though they were of a different manufacture. They found several nuts not tightened to the proper specs and four blades worn beyond repair. They circulated pictures of the damage by e-mail. As a result of this inspection they reviewed their maintenance procedures.

No less than three management acknowledgements were received complimenting Hemphill on taking and applying the learning.

On 4 April, Steve – the Salt Lake City inspector who had sent the advice – was sent the string of e-mail notes to let him see the wider benefit of him providing the recommendations, thus reinforcing the good behaviour.

Why people find time to help others

The restructuring and delayering of organizations such as BP have created flatter more business-focused companies. More gets achieved with less people. The experts sit within individual teams and businesses and are focused on delivering the objectives of their team or business. A consequence of this is that no team has the luxury of having an expert for everything they need to know. So how can we access the knowledge across the organization? We learned in the last chapter how to find out who knows, but how do we go about getting them to help and why should they?

Achieving more with less people

In the story above, the request and the solution were disseminated quickly and effectively, not to a single circulation or to a particular expert but to a series of linked, pre-existing networks. Consider how many people you know who can help you do your work inside and outside your organization? 50? If each of them knows 50 others (only half of whom are duplicate) then pretty soon you have access to a large number of people and a large amount of knowledge.

Within BP there are more than 250 networks, nobody knows exactly how many, as the number is always changing. Some are formal and have clear goals; others are very informal and help develop the capability of individuals.

Frequently the knowledge we need to do our job exists somewhere within the organization, though it is not evenly distributed. Sometimes we may not know what we don't know.

Knowledge is not evenly distributed

BP has gained a lot of value by sharing what we know as well as by importing external good practices. That value is captured by applying leading practices in a small number of our businesses.

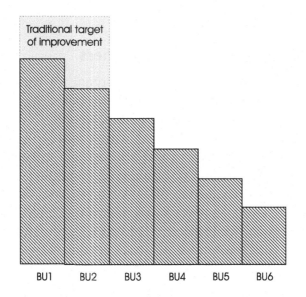

We find there is a lot more value in identifying a good practice and applying it rapidly across a large number of teams and businesses to bring each to a high standard of performance. So, imagine someone works out how to increase the productivity of a particular process that saves £10,000. If we can apply that fifty times, the company saves £500,000. We do not mandate the change; rather the network of practitioners sees the sense in making the change to improve their own performance. They would be foolish not to. They would become uncompetitive.

Quick wins come from sharing what we already know

Whilst everyone should be looking to innovate and to create new, higher standards of performance, the quick wins are likely to come from sharing what we already know somewhere in our organization.

'No traditional corporate structure, regardless of how decluttered and delayered, can muster up the speed, flexibility and focus that success today demands. Networks are faster, smarter and more flexible …'

Charan, 1991

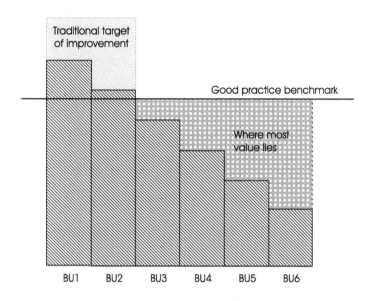

It has taken a while for us to understand how to make this happen.

> Take a few minutes to think about a time when you were effectively networking inside or outside your organization. What did success look like? How did you interact with others? How did it feel to be sharing and learning?

The life cycle of a community and definitions

Rather like the village, town or neighbourhood you live in, knowledge-sharing communities are not static. People move in and out, communities thrive and decline, share a common purpose or become fragmented. We found it useful to think of a community in terms of a life cycle; from planning, launching, through building momentum, sustaining, to closure, in order to plan our activities. We'll cover the various stages in the rest of this chapter.

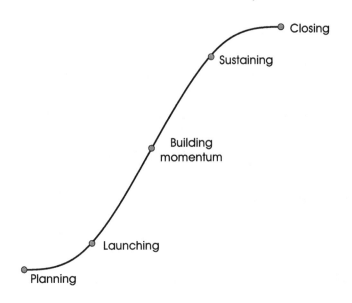

First though we would like to offer a few definitions and distinctions. We've confused ourselves frequently enough through using the same words to mean different things!

We are talking about groups of individuals sharing because they have a common interest in motorbikes; or the mutual dependency created by living on a remote island; or the spirit created by working together to respond to a challenge greater than we alone can tackle. One thing that we are not describing here is the wires that link our computers together!

Networks of people are of many different types and we give them a multitude of names. Communities operate through mutual benefit, across the normal organizational structures. At the simplest level they have few needs: a common sense of purpose, a means of communication, a good coordinator, and the autonomy to run themselves.

One classification that we have found useful is communities of interest, practice, or commitment.

- *Communities of interest* are a collection of individuals having a mutual interest in a particular topic, usually peripheral to work topics. Some examples are sports clubs, hobby groups, and charity circles.

Communities of interest, of practice and of commitment

- *Communities of practice* build and apply a practice together, agree which methods work best, and how and when they are most useful. They are the stewards of the knowledge and competence in that practice within the company. They help each other to develop the competence to contribute individually within their own department.

- *Communities of commitment* have a much harder edge. They have some clear organizational goal and the network is collectively accountable for delivery of results. Frequently these networks are a subgroup of communities of practice and have a fixed life, until what they are aiming for is delivered.

BP focuses on the second and third types of networks, and they call the communities of practice, **enabling** networks and communities of commitment, **delivery** networks.

The two types of networks are similar in many respects, but are distinguished based on the *measurable value* they provide to the business and *formality of structure*. Delivery networks have a high degree of structure to ensure we capture the high measurable value.

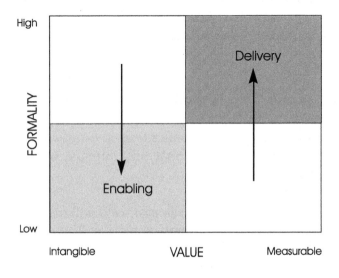

Delivering

The purpose of a *delivery network* is to deliver a common objective by pooling knowledge and translating it into actions that improve business results. BP has some clear targets on reducing greenhouse gas emissions, for example. The Green Operations network shares knowledge across the organization so the separate businesses can deliver the targeted reduction. The individuals in the network may collaborate across business boundaries.

Green Operations network

The goal of the Green Operations network is to identify, create and implement new ideas to make our operations more environmentally friendly. It facilitates company-wide communication with both managers and engineers. It currently has 575 members, some of whom are passive watchers, and a core who actively ask questions or join in the dialogue in an electronic discussion forum. There are 10–15 questions a month with an average of 6 responses to each. There is a full time facilitator who ensures that the questions are answered and that the key know-how is captured.

The network is focused around its own intranet site, which reminds them of their purpose, goals, membership and key knowledge. It is also focused by a business management steering group, who set the challenges and priorities. The Web site keeps the community aware of current issues and key projects. Knowledge transfer is also supported by specialist teams, workshops, newsletters, videos, Web casts, reports, links with academic institutions and technology companies.

BP establishes delivery networks when a significant gap between the value of current practice and recognized good practice is noticed. Capturing the full value from the network generally requires crossing organizational, disciplinary, or geographic boundaries.

The first step is to find a coordinator, who will effectively lead the group to deliver the business objective. The network has a representative business customer and also a mentor to provide assurance and coaching. The network has a performance contract with the business sponsor who may be acting on behalf of several businesses. The members of a delivery network are nominated to ensure the right expertise and representation is included.

... and enabling

Enabling networks on the other hand improve the performance of the individual members by sharing internal and external knowledge and good practices. This enables them to impact their business performance. They are defined around the *discipline* they are about, by knowledge rather than *task*. The emphasis is on building capacity for that discipline within the company. Enabling networks can be as valuable as – or more valuable than – delivery networks. However it is harder to measure that value. We have frequently found that efforts to formalize or measure the benefits jeopardize the livelihood of the network.

The three dimensional modelling (3D Mod) network is a good example of an enabling network.

3D Mod network

3D Mod is a network of practitioners of a variety of disciplines, all of who aim to understand the performance of a subsurface oil reservoir. Three-dimensional reservoir modelling is a technique to improve the detail of reservoir description, since this leads to better reservoir management. It has been running for a number of years and has a coordinator who energizes the network in his spare time. He has a full-time job delivering to one of the business units. The members rarely meet, but they help each other develop their capability to deliver within their own business. They do this by sharing what they know, and also by collectively pushing the boundaries of their shared discipline.

Most of the sharing is via a discussion group. The discussion group is a distribution list and a companion public folder on Outlook. Material posted in the folder is automatically sent to people on the distribution list. In addition the folder is open to everyone with e-mail access (all employees plus many contractors), even if they are not on the list. So an individual can choose to be prompted when there is something new, or look at the folder on an occasional basis.

'I wanted to build on a habit they had in their daily routine, the e-mail habit' says Ray. 'People can participate in the discussion or can view the contents of the forum without committing to being on the list'.

Members send messages to the folder ranging from technical queries, bug fixes, requests for help, to debates on good practices. The folder receives around 30 messages a month. Ray acts as a moderator, keeping the discussion alive and encouraging debate.

The membership is currently at 99 and, except for an increase after the BP–Amoco merger, numbers have remained steady for the last six years. There is a significant turnover of members, people join it when it is useful to them and leave it when it's not. Measured over one two-year period, half of the members changed.

After the first year or two the more than 800 messages were still in the folder, unsorted. Knowledge was becoming hard to find, and the same questions were being raised again and again. The network distilled and validated the content of the messages on a Web site, so members could look there first for frequently asked questions. This allowed the knowledge to be reused easily.

Enabling networks tend to be specialist in nature and are set up to fulfil a need when a core group is not co-located to sustain that discipline. So how do you get started?

Launching a community

Imagine you have identified some area of your business where knowledge is not evenly distributed. You may work for an educational college, which is distributed on five campuses five miles apart. You know the people at the other campuses slightly because you have met some of them irregularly in meetings. It's coming round to that time of year when the college needs to enrol students on the courses the college is offering.

Jill is in charge of enrolment. The college has clear targets for enrolment. After all, it needs to get the fees in to pay staff and cover operational costs. Jill calls a critical mass of interested parties together for a one-day meeting. Everyone with an interest in enrolment attends, including those who administer the enrolment, the curriculum managers, a representative from each subject area, and the marketing team.

Start with a meeting

In planning the meeting Jill considers the following:

1   How well do people know one another?

2   How established are the existing processes, language and good practices? Does a network already exist?

3   Are people comfortable working on shared documents from different locations?

She decides to concentrate on basic issues, such as target numbers, number of courses offered, which campuses will offer the courses. This focus will show quick results and create momentum. She allows for breaks in the meeting so people can build relationships and contacts that will subsequently lead to collaboration. She encourages collaborative problem-solving rather than sharing good practice. She finds this gets more involvement and shares good practice as a by-product (see the section on structure of peer assists in Chapter 7).

Coordinator's notes:

- *A rule of thumb is to meet face-to-face at least once a year to establish and maintain relationships. Communication can be maintained electronically but the relationship gradually decays. Meeting refreshes the relationship.*

- *Allow plenty of time for socializing in these gatherings. Avoid cramming the agenda.*

- *Sharing and collaborating with someone you know is much easier. Distributed communities depend on a core group meeting face-to-face at least once a year and are in regular contact.*

The meeting participants agree the key tasks to be completed within the timeframe and who will do what. Once the workshop is over, Jill sets up a rhythm of weekly phone conferences, and a discussion forum via an e-mail distribution list, to continue the dialogue started at the meeting. She nominates someone to coordinate the collection and sharing of all the information. Throughout the year people feel able to pick up the phone to people at other campuses to ask for help and know-how. They know who to talk to.

Coordinator's notes:

- *Provide a Web site and shared documents, such as contact details of members. This is invaluable to provide a sense of community.*

- *Shared artefacts (that is standards, shared values, a common model, procedures) play a key role. The process of creating them, and the conversations that take place to agree them, are more important than the artefacts themselves.*

- *Introduce systematic learning into network processes; that is learning before, during and after.*

Everyone is clear about the enrolment process and the part they contribute. They feel good about their successful enrolment programme. The following year they meet again, already knowing one another and build upon the processes. They prove to be faster to implement and more effective.

Networks are encouraged to develop a simple governing document, such as a terms of reference, for the benefit of the network, which includes aims and objectives, a statement of strategic value, and how it functions. See the box below for an example.

Knowledge management community terms of reference

The aim of the KM community is to deliver value to the business by increasing the effectiveness of KM practitioners around the group.

The objectives of the KM community are:

- to realize value by embedding KM practice, process and behaviour in the business;

- to provide linkages between the KM practitioners across the group thereby increasing effectiveness;

- to create a relationship between these practitioners to encourage communication;

- to provide and maintain a mechanism so that people will seek and exchange operational knowledge about the application of KM for business benefit; and

- to provide ownership, stewardship, and leadership concerning the principles of KM, as applied within the group.

Principles

The KM community will operate with a minimum of formality. It will be operationally focused, facilitated, and with membership by self-selection. Wherever possible, community members will be free and open with their questions and answers, sharing them through the community forum.

Process

The KM community will be supported by:

- a membership list;

- a discussion forum linked to e-mail;

- a Web site representing the current state of knowledge of KM; and

- a facilitator who calls meetings, manages the discussion exchanges and maintains the Web site.

This governing document may well be developed during the first face-to-face meeting and may also include roles, expectations in terms of people's time commitment and a 'code of conduct' – i.e. how members will work together.

Network coordinator

A coordinator connects not corrects

One of the keys to a successful network is the choice of coordinator (or facilitator or moderator). It does not have to be the person who calls the initial meeting. It is important that the *network coordinator* is respected by the network, is sociable, and is knowledgeable about the discipline, though preferably not *the* expert. It is better if the network members select the coordinator and she clearly operates on behalf of the network members. The role is about helping others share what they know rather than be the source of knowledge; the facilitator of the networking process rather than the fount of all knowledge.

Coordinator's notes:

- *Establish a terms of reference, or a set of objectives.*

- *Ensure lively dialogue via discussion forums by identifying people to answer unanswered questions, cross-pollinating discussion threads, and finishing responses with questions.*

- *Communicate the results and celebrate successes.*

- *Organize a regular rhythm of events.*

- *Ensure knowledge is captured, distilled, validated, shared and applied to improve organizational results.*

- *Identify and refresh membership, people leave and join according to their changing needs. Maintain distribution lists. Send personal welcome notes to new members.*

- *Act as a focal point internally and externally.*

The network coordinator may have the role full time or combine it with her existing work. Whichever option, ensure your organization recognizes it is a legitimate activity, a key contribution to the effectiveness of the company.

Members

In a large organization it is quite likely that not all the members will know each other – due to working in different locations, staff turnover or company mergers. BP uses Connect pages (see previous chapter) to make others aware of who the members are. They can list all of the members, send them an e-mail and even look at all of their photos, since it is often easier to remember a face than a name.

Recognition comes from peers and improved business performance.

We are sometimes asked about reward and recognition for network members. Does BP give financial rewards for sharing knowledge? The answer is an emphatic *no*. At BP, staff are encouraged to network when it makes sense to help business delivery. Network coordinators have their contribution explicitly reviewed as part of their annual appraisal. The reward for sharing comes from peer recognition. Those who share believe it is a powerful mechanism to improve business performance – which *is* rewarded.

Committed leadership

Networks thrive on support from senior management, to enable network activity to cross organizational boundaries. The support may come either from a sponsor or a mentor or both.

The sponsor, who is a key user of the network's output, brings a business focus, agrees a set of objectives with the network coordinator and lobbies for resources where necessary. The mentor, usually head of a particular function or discipline, provides assurance of network value, and coaching and resource support to the network.

Tools for collaboration

Today most networking occurs as a one-to-one interaction. Where the individuals are not co-located they can use a variety of collaboration tools to overcome the separation. The simple tools are the telephone and e-mail. But thinking and learning together can be more powerful. People use audio and video conferencing, and collaboration tools such as NetMeeting, to work together on a document or diagram simultaneously. If, like BP, you have people working in different time zones, then provide a shared space, and sufficient time to give people the chance to contribute to the document.

Consider how you might work collectively on a document with others rather than create a draft for comment.

How do you determine who to collaborate with? After the initial meeting, are there others you want to join? Consider whether this is for open membership or if you want to restrict membership, or if you want to screen applicants. Then send out an initial launch message to members of the network, be very clear about the purpose of the network. Create a distribution list to make it easy to address all members.

If it is an open network encourage people to send the invitation on to other people they think will be interested. Encourage a broad membership to introduce diversity of thinking. If you have a yellow-pages system (see Chapter 10) then search for people with a similar area of expertise. Search your intranet for topics connected with your domain of interest, then invite the authors to join.

Discussion forums

Online discussions with the community are a smarter way to get the right people discussing a topic rather than sending an e-mail chain, which soon irritates those who do not have an interest in the topic. The initial request or comment is sent to all members and thereafter goes to a shared space. Individuals can elect how frequently and what they receive (depending on the sophistication of the software used.) Examples of discussion forums range from the very formal, where views are screened before posting, to open chats where sometimes the advice is misleading. It really depends on the maturity of the community. Language of posting can be an issue; some discussions attempt to translate into several languages, others elect a single language for sharing. I've participated in one where the language is that of the requestor. If the topic has wider appeal then someone in the community will share a summary. In this way the conversation flows more naturally, rather like a meeting in which different preferred languages are spoken. It is for the community to decide what works and what the ground rules are.

To get an electronic discussion started we found inviting members to think of a name for the network started a democratic dialogue going.

Get the network to think of a name for themselves

Sometimes an online conference can be held around a specific topic of interest, but our experience has been that the questions posed when there is a need, bring a great discussion to the surface. What works particularly well in BP are discussions prompted by individuals in an operational site making a request for help or an offer to help. Initially you may need to prompt the behaviour of responding, and encourage people (often behind the scenes) to share their own experience, rather than offering opinions. Once people get responses to their questions within days they are encouraged to ask more. And as you saw in the opening example, others benefit from the responses too.

Networks are mainly self-sustaining but they can benefit from some help and resources. Initially, BP had a central knowledge management team. It encouraged the development and improvement of networks. It provided guidance and resources when needed, helped communities connect their agenda to business strategies. The KM team encouraged and challenged the networks, making sure the right people were included, and helped with links to other, similar networks.

Here is an example of a coordinator who works at a global scale. Marlou is an experienced e-facilitator, or moderator, of electronic networks in the field of HIV and AIDS. She works for a United Nations agency but the networks she facilitates spread across the organizational boundaries and across the world.

Marlou expresses the essence of networking as 'a feeling you are not alone, that others are struggling with the same issues as you, and that maybe some can help you. An opportunity to share what you know and learn, and a chance to learn things that you didn't know you didn't know.'

The networking you see on the surface is only the tip of the iceberg. There is so much more happening than you can read in the exchange on an electronic discussion. People contact each other after they have read the posting. For example Jennie read a posting while she was in Uganda and at that time had nothing to comment. Some time later she was visiting Zambia on another matter and decided to visit one of the contributors to the discussion. They exchanged ideas on local response to AIDS and Jennie used these in her next activity in Uganda.

> The networking you see on the surface is only the tip of the iceberg.

There are a rising number of people dying with AIDS, and we still do not have the tools to eradicate AIDS or to improve the quality of life for those living with AIDS. Further, there is a lack of access locally to basic information about how people develop AIDS, and hence can avoid it. Several people from different countries and backgrounds got together for a meeting on 'How to build partnerships to support local responses' in Bulawayo, Zimbabwe. To start with it was the usual formal presentation and questions format. Then they went on a field visit together and during that informal time together they exchanged a lot. People got to know each other, they were energized. At the end of the meeting people were looking for ways to continue the discussion in an informal setting, so approximately 25 people started an electronic discussion using a list server. Each of them deliberately invited others they knew and thought would contribute. They introduced themselves to each other – who they were, their interests, what they were working on and so on.

Initially the topics for discussion were agreed between moderators in the office and then posed, but it felt very artificial. Then people started to ask questions – things they really needed to

People started to ask questions – things they really needed to know

know, that was when it took on a life of its own.

Over four years the 25 people have grown to 670. What made it grow? After deliberately building it to a 100, the subsequent increase has been by word of mouth (or more accurately *word of e-mail!*) Turnover of members is about 4% since it started.

The local response is a broad topic and different subgroups have different interests, Marlou notices this when for instance a topic on youth comes up, there is a certain set of frequent participants. Of course not all participants are visible - readers participate too. Marlou estimates about 10% of the 670 members are *really* active.

One of her challenges is to make new entrants feel welcome and at ease coming into a new community. It's rather like coming late into a large roomful of people who have already spent time together; you look around for someone or something familiar, otherwise you take a seat in the far corner and keep quiet until you meet someone in the break. It maybe the tool is new to them and certainly the electronic space is somewhere they haven't been before. It takes a while to find their way around.

The best way to make them feel comfortable is if they see a question in from the field, from a real person with a real need that they can identify with. Much of what Marlou contributes has been learned by experience.

'Don't touch the way questions are phrased', she cautions.

Typically the first responses come from people known to Marlou, one's she has visited or met in meetings, 'friends' setting a good example, and then others feel encouraged and confident to share, people not personally known to Marlou. A core group of friends is important, and the e-facilitator needs to know these people.

Make it as informal as possible. Formality kills the flow, so encourage different experiences, and live with contradictions. Formal policy statements tend to end the thread of a conversation. End an e-mail with a question to the community.

> End an e-mail with a question to the community

> Can you recall a time when a lively discussion came to an abrupt end? What could you have done to continue the flow?

Coordinator's notes: When a discussion stops, rephrase questions that came up in earlier contributions but were not answered. Make interim summaries and ask if this accurately reflects people's experience. Often at this stage new people will come in to add different experiences.

Another approach Marlou has used is to pick up the phone to a random selection of the network, be honest and tell people there is not enough response and ask what would make it work for them, what topics, what could make it easier, and what is preventing them from participating now? Encourage them to respond to the next e-mail you send. In the development world not everyone has daily access to a computer, some must travel miles to reach an internet café. Electronic discussions do require that people read their e-mail regularly – not necessarily everyday – but often enough to provide a timely contribution.

Marlou cautions that the electronic discussion forum is only one of the ways of communicating.

> *'Consider using the telephone, face-to-face meetings, e-mail, the Web and CD-ROM as complementary ways of communicating with networks and consider which is appropriate for the occasion.'*

Build momentum

What can we do to build momentum once a network has been formed, to ensure the initial enthusiasm when people meet together is maintained when they are apart? Here are some ideas that have worked well for us:

- Send a welcoming e-mail to new members or a telephone call and introduce them to other members in their location. We share with those we *know* and *trust*, so get to know the members.

- Publicise the network in your organization's magazine and intranet so that others are aware it exists. Even if people don't see a need to join it, they'll know where to direct people and when to exchange between networks on shared topics.

- Establish the right behaviours by asking a question on behalf of a member (or preferably have the members do it themselves) and press for answers behind the scenes if they are not quickly forthcoming.

- Advertise quick wins. When questions get answered and people make good use of the response, publish the successes, rather like the story at the start of this chapter. It encourages other questions and responses.

- Monitor the activity of the discussion forum – some possible indicators are frequency of contribution, frequency of response, number of unanswered questions, number of joiners and leavers, Web site, or document access. Watch out for any significant changes in trends.

- Maintain connectivity, through regular teleconferences, newsletter, shared team space or Web site. Keeping a regular rhythm of events helps people remember the network is there, and remember socializing by teleconference is as important as the agenda as it allows collaboration to be effective between meetings.

Being part of the community

So what does it feel like to be part of a network? When someone calls me to ask for some advice I feel valued and trusted. When I ask for help from others and get several timely responses I feel part of something larger than

Having your answer listened to raises self-esteem

my immediate team. I enjoy the relationship I have with others in the community. People I encounter are passionate about what they are doing and what they know. I trust the know-how I get because I either know the person supplying it because I met them in a workshop last year, or I know someone else who knows them. I am confident that the person who made an offer will do what they said they would.

I have a sense that I have made real progress because I have achieved something in my work that I could not have achieved alone. And I have saved time doing it; time that I can use to do something else. In short, I feel a valued member of the community.

Members of networks tend to have peer recognition and are actively practising. They are good communicators and are active listeners. They are committed to improving the performance of the whole organization not just the performance of their immediate team.

Sustaining the network

There comes a time when all questions have been answered, or the same questions are being asked again, and the network exists in name but the interaction drops off. People know one another well enough that they go directly to someone who can help. What can you do to enliven the network and renew commitment?

We've used the following approaches:

- Refine the membership, by sending an e-mail to existing members reminding them to let you know if they want to be removed from the list. It is much better to have a small group of committed members than a larger number with varied commitment.

- Call a face-to-face meeting on a current issue. Consider regional meetings if cost is an issue. At the end of the meeting agree some actions to sustain the conversation.

- Keep the focus on the key organizational issues, as if topics shared are not relevant to the majority then they will turn off. Publicize more success stories relating to how someone received help from the network and created something valuable as a result.

- Review the performance of the network against the terms of reference or performance contract. Ask 'Why?', if it has under performed, and don't forget: celebrate success if it *has* performed. This can be something simple like an acknowledgement in the organizations in-house magazine, or a letter from the boss. Consider redefining the deliverables and scope; if the network is large consider making sub networks so the topic is more relevant.

Don't be afraid to close the network

- Ultimately, don't be afraid to close the network. The threat alone will test the members need for it to continue. Close it by celebrating the successes, acknowledge the key contributors, then move on to make a difference, to deliver results, elsewhere.

Communities as the stewards of the company's knowledge

Where does the knowledge reside in your organization? We've talked about knowledge being in knowledge stores – as electronic and paper documents and maybe as audio and videotapes.

> The community keeps the knowledge alive

Far more of it is in the heads of people working in the organization. Networks are the best way we have found to create, shape and realize value from knowledge. They are key in validating and distilling know-how in their practice area. Knowledge does not remain static. It's not a case of storing a document on a shelf and leaving it to gather dust. The community has a role to play in adding to it, using it, deleting it when appropriate, distilling it and building it into business processes. Through sharing ideas, tips and hints, problems and solutions, they are able to access the knowledge of the whole community so that each individual can operate more effectively.

You've heard it said that no one is indispensable. This will be true only if the network shares its knowledge so no one person holds unique knowledge. Many of BP's networks build Web pages, which hold the latest view of the knowledge of that practice area. They have a multitude of good-practice databases. Today those Web pages and those databases 'die' when the owner moves. If the community *really* embraces building these knowledge assets, then they save the company's knowledge from dependency on individuals. – see Chapter 12, Leveraging What We've Learned – Capturing Knowledge, for more insights on this topic.

The United Nations Development Programme (UNDP) have devised an effective combination of global network and regional resource teams to ensure their knowledge and experience reaches the people who need it. UNDP brings together governments, civil society, multinational corporations and multilateral organizations on particular issues of concern (from politics to public health, from crime to the environment) and looks for ways to address them.

UNDP offers its clients a knowledge-based advisory service based on networks of twelve practice areas such as the one on democratic governance and nine regional policy consultancies called SURFs, which support clusters of countries in the region. In other words the expertise is decentralized and closer to the action. It is structured to provide clients with the most immediate and effective response.

> 'Country office staff are better equipped to tackle the full range of development challenges, knowing they are backed up by, and able to access our global team of specialists.'
> Mark Malloch Brown, Administrator, UNDP

Guaranteeing a response from the network

One striking feature is that they *guarantee* a response to a request from a country office. The effect of this is that there are more questions asked and also more willingness to share experience from around the world. More than half of UNDP's staff, over 4000 people from every part and from all levels of the worldwide organization, participate in one or more networks. As people find it helps them do their work they are more likely to ask again, and at the same time reciprocate.

In recent weeks the Guyana Country office has requested the support of the SURF in fulfilling several critical and time-sensitive requests for information from the Government of Guyana.

We received word yesterday from the Office of the President as to the value of the information you helped us to gather. They were particularly happy with the references to legislation, copies of reports and so on, and wished to communicate their gratitude to UNDP for the thoroughness and depth of the information unearthed.

We fully expect to continue relying on the SURF in the future for this valuable support.

Jan Sorensen, UNDP Resident Representative, Guyana

So what happened to receive such a response?

In October 2003 a request was received by the Caribbean SURF to provide examples of model legislation for a government in their region regarding parliamentarians 'crossing the floor' i.e. leaving one political party and joining another. The reply was distilled from experience offered from around the world and from the SURFs who use their policy specialists for in depth research. Within days, responses were received from the American Bar Association (ABA), the UNDP Headquarters, and from UNDP offices in Uzbekistan, Sri Lanka, Nepal and Zambia, and the knowledge network facilitator made a consolidated reply six days after the request was received. The reply included the fact that model legislation could be found in eight countries, and electronic links were offered to the legislation. The ABA offered case studies and a research summary. The consolidation finished with a summary of pros and cons of legislation to consider.

Consolidate the reply

The structure of the consolidated reply is worth sharing:

- It states the query as a headline, and includes the original e-mail request.

- It lists who the responses are from.

- It summarizes responses in less than a page.

- It lists and links to related resources and the e-mail addresses of relevant people to contact.

- It lists the responses in full.

- It invites others to add to the response.

I asked Deodat Maharaj of the Caribbean SURF what are some of the key lessons learned by UNDP from this approach? He replied 'Firstly, quality and relevant responses are ensured by carefully phrasing the request. Secondly, tapping into our global knowledge can swiftly facilitate the finding of development solutions and thirdly, the connection through regional SURFs having familiarity with the local context is key to a relevant response.'

The UNDP Country office feels able to answer any query of a government by tapping directly into the decentralized network of policy advisors and the global experience of UNDP. The approach offers speed (six days to accumulate knowledge that might take a government months), quality and neutrality. By delivering on this service UNDP is positioned as trusted partner.

In this chapter we have explored why people are prepared to find the time to help others and how they do it. We've looked at communities for spreading the company's knowledge more evenly. We have discussed what it takes to launch and to sustain these communities and finally we've examined their role as stewards of the company's knowledge.

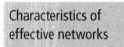 **Characteristics of effective networks**

We believe networks are essential in a flat organization to share the company's know-how widely. The most effective networks share the following characteristics:

- Select a coordinator or moderator carefully to manage the network processes and create a rhythm of interactions.

- Have a sponsor who makes clear what the business needs, supports by finding resources and who speaks powerfully about the intent of the network.

- Have their experts decentralized but connected.

- Have clear enabling mechanisms to sustain the interactions, methods such as intranet community pages, electronic discussion forums and shared tools and artefacts.

- Respond rapidly to a request for knowledge.

- Synthesize the responses from a discussion so they can be reused. Act as stewards for the organization's knowledge.

- Meet physically occasionally so the members get to know one another.

- Have a clear, simple governing document, either a perform- ance contract or a terms of reference. Get clear whether the network is developing the capability and competency of the organization or is focused on delivering something with *measurable* value.

- Act empowered, are proactive, add value, and save time.

Marlou looks forward to the day when networks are self-moder- ating, when the facilitator does not need to be there any longer, to when the people in the network are taking the initiative to update and synthesize their own knowledge assets and having a big party to build relationships and make it easier for people to follow up on discussions one to one. She believes the community should be a fun place, and draws an analogy with a recent meet- ing she attended in Dakar.

> *'There was a place outside the meeting rooms, a place where people were offering food in the open air, people from all backgrounds were sitting around on carpets eating and having animated conversations. It was very informal and natural - some day all networks will be like this!'*

Why not find out what it is like to be part of a virtual community of practice on the topic of knowledge management? Join your fellow readers now at: http://www.learning-to-fly.org

In this chapter:

- Why it is important to capture knowledge.

- How to make captured knowledge accessible through 'knowledge assets'.

- How to capture an event or key meeting in a way that involves everybody.

- How to capture knowledge from someone leaving their current role.

A powerful story from the US Army

Professor John Henderson from Boston University once told a powerful story about the US Army to a gathering of senior BP managers. Before he started the story, he asked whether BP had any formal approach to capturing strategic knowledge. The chief engineer raised his hand and described a database of 'project lessons learned'. John acknowledged this, and went on to tell this story:

'I interviewed a colonel. Now this colonel was a colonel in the 82nd airborne, one of the more elite groups in the US Army. He got a call on Saturday morning at 8 o'clock reminding him that

a hurricane had just hit. He was told that because the current administration had very strong ties to that particular part of the country that they did not believe that this should be left to the reserve group because they wanted "no screw-ups".

'So the orders to the colonel were very clear: go down there, provide any support necessary to the people after this hurricane and don't screw up. Clear orders. The army calls it intent - strategic intent. The strategic intent was clear.

'This particular colonel was a very highly decorated combat soldier - he had never done this in his life. He had never actually commanded any type of civilian-related activity. He'd always been right on the front lines in hot action. It turns out as part of the executive education in the army he had been exposed to the 'Centre for Army Lessons Learned' as part of their executive education process.

'So he got on his laptop computer he dialled into Army net, hooked into the Centre for Army Lessons Learned and asked the following question - he actually showed me the type:

'"What does the Army know about hurricane clean-up?"

'Within four hours he had:

- *A profile of the deployment of troops in the last three hurricanes that occurred in North America that the army was sent to provide support and clean-up including types of staff, types of skills, numbers of skills.*

- *A pro-forma budget – both what budget was required and what the actual budget was and where the cost overruns were.*

- *The ten questions that you will be asked by CNN in the first 30 minutes on your arrival.*

- *A list of every state agency and federal agency that had to be contacted and coordinated with and the name of the person that he had to contact, and the army liaison person who was currently working with that group some place in North America.*

- *Established a Lotus Notes advisory team of the three commanders, who agreed to be his advisory group in this command structure.*

Then John Henderson asked: 'Is this of relevance to British Petroleum?'

A pregnant pause followed, after which the chief engineer again raised his hand.

> *'You asked whether we had a formal approach to capturing knowledge? Well, we have nothing, nothing at all that is anything like that!'*

Why capture knowledge in the first place?

We talked about BP's bias for connecting people rather than capturing knowledge, and we talked of the value of the ten-minute phone call. But what happens when the same person gets a ten-minute phone call from tens or hundreds of people about the same topic? What if she is not available when you need to know? What if there are ten people you need to talk to rather than just one? Then it may be the time to capture and package knowledge for reuse.

Many people hold the view that the moment that something becomes codified – written down, physically or electronically – at that moment it becomes mere information and consequently loses value. True 'knowledge' is bound up in the context of the person telling the story, and you can't separate one from the other ...

In his book *Silent Messages*, Albert Mehrabian suggests that in any communication, roughly 7 per cent of the message is in the words, 38 per cent is in the tone of the voice, and the remaining 55 per cent of the message is communicated in body language. If this suggestion bears out, then we lose 93 per cent of the message – the context – when we reduce someone telling a story to a simple textual document.

> Loss of context when capturing knowledge as information

In an ideal world, we would all share knowledge face-to-face, and would never need to capture anything. The only difficulty here is that none of us are omnipresent! We can't be everywhere at once, so what's needed is a way to represent knowledge in a way that makes sense to others without losing too much of that context.

The challenge to learn, and the practical challenge of 'when to stop'...

But even that's not enough – how many stories are you prepared to read before you feel that you've learned enough? Five? Ten? Or just one or two that seem to justify what you've already planned to do?

That's the trouble. We struggle to absorb all the information available to us, and yet still don't feel knowledgeable.

These days everyone complains about information overload, but you never hear anyone complaining about 'knowledge overload'.

Tell me the ten things I need to know

In BP, the heartfelt plea of many people has been 'I don't have time to read all these reports – just tell me the ten things that I really need to know.'

So there's the challenge: we need to capture knowledge in a way that retains as much context as possible so that we can multiply its benefit. However, sometimes too much *specific* context can cloud our judgement as to how transferable a particular piece of knowledge is. To avoid a premature 'it'll never work here' problem, it is important to distil the key learning themes out from the details, so that people quickly find their way to the most salient points – and *then* decide where they are relevant.

Imagine that you are watching TV, and have just seen a celebrity wearing a particularly fashionable suit. The way they walk, their accessories, the place they are seen in, the company they are seen with – all of these factors might persuade you that you could never look *that* good in a similar suit, and you wouldn't contemplate buying it. Let's face it, it would probably cost a four or five figure sum! If however you walked into your favourite clothing store, and saw that suit on a mannequin or on a hanger (and the price was right) – you might try it on. It's the same suit – just presented in more neutral environment – arranged with a customer in mind. *As a person responsible for capturing and packaging knowledge, your challenge is to carefully put the examples back onto the 'clothes hangers' as guidelines with a wider appeal.*

Thinking back to the US Army hurricane example. What was it that was so powerful about John's story? Everyone could identify with the colonel being set a task that he didn't know how accomplish. What were the elements that we could learn from, and bring into, our own environment?

- Actual documents and plans used in previous hurricane clean-up exercises.

- Access to exactly the right detail of information where it was needed – the actual and planned budgets for each previous event, and the profile of troops deployed.

- Access to people – key contacts and relationships with precisely the right people who had a commitment to help him as a 'real-time' virtual advisory team.

- Access to summarized, critical points – such as the first ten questions that CNN might ask – something the colonel might not have known to ask for.

- All within four hours of asking one simple question.

On the basis of that story, BP's knowledge management team worked to create a framework for capturing knowledge that incorporated these principles – we gave that framework the name 'knowledge asset', and set about learning how to create and sustain it inside the company.

Repeatable processes eliminate repeatable mistakes

Much of what BP does is repeated in one way or another. They build petrol stations in Venezuela, then Japan, then Poland. Each of these actions generates its own story - its own record of what happened, what the context was, what lessons were learned. After a short time, this library of stories begins to build. Staff in Japan read what happened in Venezuela, put that experience to work locally, and create their own story.

Distillation makes knowledge more accessible

Over time, the volume of reading material could increase dramatically, much as people like reading stories, there are practical limits. This is where the value of *distillation* comes through. Consistent patterns begin to emerge that are common across the stories - Venezuela, Japan, Poland - these patterns then form the basis of a set of key guidelines as part of a knowledge asset.

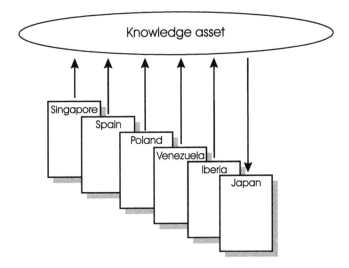

BP is a global energy company, and a large part of our business comes from the discovery and processing of crude oil.

Some crudes are tar-like in their consistency, others are far less viscous - in all cases, the oil itself is a tremendously complex cocktail of components. No two crudes are ever chemically the same, but most of them smell unpleasant!

We employ some very smart people who have the skills and the technology to analyse samples of crude oil and then character-ize their properties – each one having a unique 'fingerprint' that indicates the likely constituents into which it might be sepa-rated. Crude Oil Assay – the technical term for this work – is a highly skilled job, done by just a few people.

However, we don't create useful products from crude oil by analysis – we distil it on an enormous scale, into its commercially viable components, at refineries. Large fractionating columns subject the oil to the right combination of pressure and tem-perature, and the simple, refined products are distilled off at various points – refinery gas, LPG, gasoline, heavy fuel oil, and so on. Anyone working at that part of the refinery could point out to you the product extracted at that stage – whether it went in your car engine, or the fuel tank.

Let's move on from the distillation of crude oil and think about the analogy for capturing and packaging knowledge.

Whilst the laboratory expert could characterize and accurately describe the components of a crude oil sample, it didn't really have utility until the component parts were separated and made accessible by the process of distillation. At that point, the value can be realized, and these components can become the basis of other commercial products.

Think about day-to-day business in your organization. Some-where in the complex mixture of experiences, relationships, conversations and documents lie some simple powerful insights – insights which have commercial value and should be made easily accessible to others. So the trick is to take that mixture and distil it into a reusable set of lessons, which can be accessed and explored by others in the organization. Lessons that instantly answer the question 'What are the first ten things which I need to know?'

The ProduceCo* mergers and acquisitions knowledge asset

ProduceCo is a leading manufacturer and supplier of brand-name consumer goods, operating in the global marketplace and supplying well-known consumer products to retailers and supermarkets. ProduceCo has been investigating knowledge management, as a way of supporting corporate growth.

In the summer of 2002, Sarah, the leader of the Knowledge Management (KM) team in ProduceCo, was looking to try out some KM tools in the organization. She wanted to see what would work in their corporate culture, and to assess whether KM had the potential to make a difference to the way their employees operate. One of the tools that caught Sarah's eye was the knowledge asset. What is more, she had an excellent opportunity to build a knowledge asset – ProduceCo had just completed the acquisition of a small producer of specialist products, and the acquisitions team had gained considerable knowledge of 'How to conduct an acquisition'.

Sarah felt that capturing and packaging the knowledge from this acquisition would have several benefits to ProduceCo:

- It would allow the KM tools of retrospect, interview and knowledge asset to be tried out.

- It would (if successful) provide a showcase knowledge asset which could be used to engage the organization in KM.

- It would capture strategic knowledge, which would help the organization in future acquisitions.

Sarah brought in Nick Milton, of Knoco Ltd, to work with her in constructing the knowledge asset. Sarah and Nick held a retrospect for the core acquisitions team, and added to this with interviews from several of the other key players, including several very senior members of the organization. The material from the interviews and retrospect were arranged into themes, and compiled into a

*ProduceCo is a fictitious name.

knowledge asset. The knowledge was organized into '120 questions you need to address when acquiring another company', with each question answered in the words of the acquisitions team.

The pilot project was very successful. It allowed Sarah to try out the tools and concepts, and knowledge assets have now been adopted as one of the components of the official 'Knowledge Management Toolkit'. The knowledge contained in the asset was proven to be of great value, and the leader of the acquisitions team requested that the asset be updated a year later, after several more acquisitions and divestments. The knowledge asset now answers 200 questions, with answers from 18 contributors, and with major new sections on post-acquisition integration, and divestment.

In some ways, it was too successful! The knowledge is considered so important for ProduceCo, and so strategic, that the acquisitions team prefer to restrict access to the knowledge asset. Sarah was therefore unable to use it as a showcase example. So there are some lessons here for KM implementation! Although the acquisition was a very good opportunity for KM (in that it was recent, a lot of knowledge had been gained, and the contributors were at a very high level in the organization, thus giving credibility to the process), in another way it was too strategic and too sensitive to provide a showcase example. Sarah has since needed to capture knowledge in some less sensitive areas, to be able to develop a knowledge asset she can share with the rest of the organization.

Nick Milton

Here are the ten steps for creating a knowledge asset that have been tried and tested in some of BP's most critical knowledge areas.

Guidelines for building a knowledge asset

1   Is there a customer for this knowledge?

Have a clear customer – current or future – in mind when considering the creation of a

Ten steps towards creating a knowledge asset

knowledge asset. Without a customer, you may be creating a 'knowledge graveyard'. Who has, or will have a need to know something? Even if the requirement for this knowledge is not immediate, think about the needs of a *potential* future customer.

For example, perhaps have the opportunity to gather insights from a series of mergers or acquisitions. Even if the next merger is months or years away, put yourself in the place of the person leading such an activity. What would make this knowledge asset invaluable to that person?

2 Are you clear what your knowledge asset is really about?

What is the scope of your knowledge asset? What will it be called?

A knowledge asset needs to cover a specific, and not too broad, area of business activity.

Examples of knowledge assets in BP include:

- 'Conducting a turnaround at a refinery.'

- 'Transferring ownership of an offshore platform.'

- 'Restructuring and right-sizing our business.'

Which topics would be most valuable to your organization? What are the strategically important, repeatable events that would really make a difference in your organization?

You need to get some idea of what the content of the knowledge asset will be. Try this. Ask yourself:

- 'What do I need to know in order to do business?'

- 'What is the biggest issue facing me today?'

- 'Do I need to know processes, techniques, people, reasons for acting?'

- 'Do I need know-who, know-what and know-why in addition to know-how?'

- 'Why bother? What difference would it will make if I didn't capture this knowledge?'

3   Is there a community of practice relating to this subject?

Knowledge assets should be owned by communities of practice, who regularly refresh the content to keep it current. The community will be the source of the knowledge in the first place, the users of the knowledge in future, and the people who validate the knowledge in the knowledge asset. For example, the asset 'how to drill effectively in deep water' is owned by the drilling engineers. If there is no existing community of practice, you should try to establish one - in fact, the very process of collating history and exchanging knowledge may be a powerful catalyst to bringing the community together.

Communities of practice are the guardians of knowledge assets

4 Is there existing material upon which you can base your knowledge asset?

Gather what's already there

Often, someone in the company will have made efforts to record lessons or recommendations in some form – this will be important content to incorporate into your knowledge asset. Your first step will be to collate the existing material. This may include:

- lessons-learned reports and project-completion reports;

- the results of any After Action Reviews or retrospects;

- interviews with key players;

- researching important documents and artefacts, such as project plans, communications plans, sample presentations, project processes, etc.; and

- if you are working in a new area, you may need to conduct interviews and introduce some learning processes such as After Action Reviews (see Chapter 8) and retrospects (see Chapter 9), in order to generate the content for the knowledge asset. Additionally you could consider the wealth of information that exists beyond your company's walls, either from the Internet, or other external sources.

Provide a distillation of the key messages

OK, you're half way there. Make yourself a generous cup of coffee, take a deep breath, lock the door and immerse yourself.

5 Look for the general principles or guidelines

Provide some context so that people can understand the purpose and relevance of the knowledge asset. What was the business environment when this was created? Why was this seen as important at the time? Who brought this material together?

A knowledge asset works as a general guide for future use in all contexts. Go through the historical records of previous work and extract the knowledge from the context in which it sits. Different people will have seen certain approaches work at certain times.

Are there general guidelines that you can distil out of this material?

The distillation is a creative and value-adding step – probably the most important one. You are taking what may be a mass of material, and distilling it out into something really useful. It doesn't have to be a solo effort, but it is not something that you would engage a large group to try and do. In all cases, it will require a block of uninterrupted time (a day or more in most cases), space, your undivided attention and a set of coloured marker pens.

6 Build a checklist illustrated with examples and stories

The checklist should tell the user of the knowledge asset:

- 'What are the questions I need to ask myself?'

> Checklists, rule-books and question sets

- 'What are the top ten things that I need to think about?'

- 'What is the information that I need to gather?'

- 'What are the steps that I need to take?'

How you present this checklist is entirely up to the customer. Some people seem to respond better to a set of questions (e.g. 'Have you considered using a facilitator?') than they do to a set of rules and procedures (e.g. 'Use a facilitator where appropriate'), whilst others will prefer to work to a 'rule book'. Check which style is preferred, rather than risk distracting or irritating the reader.

Check with your community of practice as to which format people prefer.

If the topic is a part of a recognized process, consider structuring the guidelines in a way which mirrors the process steps. This will mean that the knowledge asset can be used as reference material to support anyone working through these steps, acting as a form of e-learning.

Stories and quotes bring knowledge back to life

Checklists generally read as dry and academic, and it helps if you illustrate them with examples, stories, pictures, models, quotes, video and audio clips, if possible. Get agreement from the individual referenced, and make sure that they are happy with sharing their quote or clip more widely.

It can also be valuable to include links to important source documents, so the reader can follow things up further if they want or use them as a template. For example, BP's knowledge asset on 'Business Restructuring' includes project plans, communications strategies, presentation materials and briefing documents.

From the reader's perspective, they will usually access the knowledge assets via the checklist, and drill-down into the areas which interest them, through key quotes, as far as in-depth transcripts, video clips and these key documents.

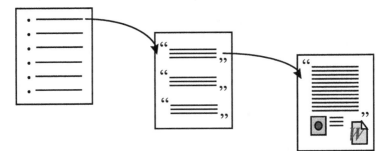

This book is an example of this structured approach. You can move from a high-level list in the table of contents, through to a more detailed description of each chapter, or into the chapter content itself.

7 Emphasize links to people

Although the knowledge asset will include a lot of explicit knowledge, there will be far more knowledge still residing in the heads of the community of practice as tacit knowledge.

Point to people – the most valuable asset

This knowledge is also a vital part of the knowledge asset and it is important to point to it wherever possible. Create a hyperlink to the person's personal homepage or e-mail address wherever you mention them in the text. Include a list of all the people with any relationship with the content – their photograph, e-mail address, telephone number and a link to any personal homepage (see Chapter 10, Finding the Right People). The photograph is significant, as it is psychologically much easier to contact someone if you know what they look like.

Make sure you include your name and contact details (and photograph, if you like) at the bottom of the page. Additionally, provide details of the community of practice – who leads it, access to a discussion forum or mailing list.

8 Validate the guidelines

You will have constructed a knowledge asset, with guidelines based on history and experience collected from the community of practice. The next step should be to circulate it around the community again, and ask, 'do the guidelines accurately reflect your knowledge and experience?' and 'do you have anything to add?'

Validation comes from the community

9 Publish the knowledge asset

You now need to make the explicit part of the knowledge asset widely available, so that the community of practice can access it at any time. If the content is sensitive – and the openness and frankness of some of the content may increase its sensitivity – then you may find that you have to restrict access. Don't worry too much about this; the community is your primary audience; they will be the people who apply the guidelines and create value through its application. You will just have to look else-where for a showcase example that you can share around the entire organization!

Select the right medium for publishing knowledge

Where you put it will depend on the nature of this community. The knowledge asset has to 'live with its owners'. For a local community this might be something as simple as an office wall, and for a global, or virtual community of practice, that means you will probably store the knowledge in virtual space – typically on the intranet. The power of the hyper-link means that original documents can reside with their owners, and just be linked to, from the knowledge asset.

Of course, you don't have to restrict yourself to a single medium. In the BP Norway office, the results of retrospects were put on the notice board by the coffee machines, where all the impor-tant managerial notices were posted. Everyone browsed this board daily, and the retrospect output was printed on bright coloured paper to catch the eye. The lessons were also sorted and put on the intranet, but posting them on the board was a key step in making them visible.

If the knowledge asset is a local one, serving a local community, then you could store it in physical space rather than electroni-cally. An example of this would be the 'war room' that BP Viet-nam set up as part of their knowledge management program. This was a room where people could gather before and after negotiations with the government, where they could hold After Action Reviews (AARs) and share what they knew. It held a large chart on the wall that was updated after every meeting, and held a filing cabinet in the corner containing the records of all the AARs.

10   Finally, keep it alive – initiate a feedback and ownership process

When you publish the knowledge asset, make sure there is a visible feedback mechanism so that users can validate through use. You will want to encourage feedback from users, so that they pick up and eliminate any invalid recommendations. Make sure there is some sort of maintenance mechanism. Instil a sense of obligation that 'if you use it, then you should add to it'. Responsibility for maintenance may lie with the facilitator for the community (network leader or similar). Alternatively, this responsibility can move from one business unit to another as activity migrates within the business.

For example, the knowledge asset for deep-water drilling was created initially by the Gulf of Mexico business unit, then used by Scottish Foinaven field, updated by them then used by its neighbour, Schiehallion. Similarly, it could make sense if the refinery currently running a turnaround took ownership of the 'turnarounds' knowledge, making sure it was complete before, and updated after, the exercise.

In a way, it's a little like carrying the Olympic torch - keeping the flame burning for the next team.

One way of reinforcing the link between the knowledge asset, and the actual business events, is to include a 'news' section on the Web site, where you can list future events. The 'Refinery Turnarounds' knowledge asset does exactly this, listing a timetable of future turnarounds for refineries around with world. This builds awareness in the community of practice, and increases the likelihood that the content will be used at the time when it most useful.

There's a danger that this all sounds like a simple recipe - one that can be guaranteed to create the perfect result every time.

The reality is that sustaining a knowledge asset is more difficult than creating it in the first place.

Sustaining a knowledge asset is the toughest part

Our experience is that success hinges on the active presence of a community of practice who feel a strong sense of ownership for the content. Without that, the result can be an elegant Web site ... that rapidly falls into disrepair and becomes a monument to some fine research. Alternatively, an individual takes editorial charge of the knowledge asset, and religiously maintains it, but fails to take into consideration the opinions of the rest of the community.

Unfortunately, it's easier to create a company expert than to sustain a company-wide community.

The result in this case can be a testimony to that individual's expert opinion, rather than the shared view of a group of people who act collectively as stewards of the company's intellectual capital. This is the difference between one person declaring what they do as 'good practice', rather than good practice being acclaimed by a group of people.

Moving towards good practices

Initially, what gets captured in knowledge assets are *practices* – successful ways of working that are applied somewhere inside the organization. Sometimes these are applied by other businesses and can be called *common practices*. Occasionally, *good practices* emerge from these common practices, as adoption 'snowballs' and a community of practice validates and recommends a practice.

Knowledge assets and communities as mechanisms for identifying good practices

The ease with which good practices emerge is a reflection of the culture in the organization. Where a 'not invented here' culture is prevalent, practices remain in the 'outer ring', as each business defends its own way of operating, rather than learning from others.

Where staff are encouraged to seek out knowledge, whether in knowledge assets or in the heads of other individuals, then good practices are more likely to emerge. The existence of a knowledge asset will raise awareness of what practices exist, and the presence of community of practice serves to accelerate the process of validation and widespread adoption of good practices.

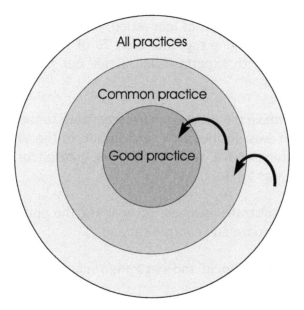

How do practices move between the different categories in your organization? Ask yourself:

- 'Is there a natural "gravity" which draws practices towards the centre, or a not-invented-here "centripetal force" which keeps them at the periphery?'

- 'What could you do to change the impact of these forces at the interfaces of each boundary?'

Capturing the essence of a key event

How do you capture the essence of a signifi-cant event, so that people who didn't attend in person can feel as though they participated?

For your organization, perhaps, this might be a product launch, a shareholder meeting or an annual general meeting?

Creating a management event for the whole organization, then capturing it for the future organization

In the late 1990s, BP held an internal meeting (known as a col-loquium) on the subject of innovation. It was a major meeting, and involved bringing together over 70 of the company's top management with experts from outside our industry for two intensive days.

In order to make the meeting more accessible to the rest of the company, it was decided that, in addition to the VHS video of the presenters, a 'live' Web site would be created for the event. The intent was twofold:

- to demonstrate openness by enabling the entire company to participate and contribute; and

- to capture a vivid and engaging record of the event for future reference.

The Web site was created, and a team posted an extract of each session onto the Web site approximately every two hours. The extract included photographs, sound bites, transcripts of key quotes, and a journalistic summary of the discussion or presenta-tion in question, headed by a catchy or provocative title.

Additionally, feedback, ideas and challenges from the entire company were solicited via e-mail, and a summary of 'what the company is saying' was brought into the room and worked by the senior managers present. It was a truly inclusive process.

The feedback from the virtual participants was tremendous:

> *'Greetings to you all from Thistle A – a very mature asset in the Northern North Sea. We are all avid readers of the site and think it is an excellent idea – innovation itself! We look forward to visiting the site over the next few days and we thank you for the opportunity to give input. Team Thistle'*
>
> Collective contribution from the crew of an oil rig in the North Sea
>
> *'This is a great example of innovation, encompassing people, process and technology! It is enabling people way beyond the walls of Durdent Court to feel able to participate. I'm accessing this today in Anchorage and next week I'll be dipping in from deep in the Sahara Desert. This is sharing what we know and learn on a grand scale!'*
>
> Business consultant in Alaska

In today's world, where entire rock concerts are regularly Webcasted to a potential audience of millions via the Internet, this all sounds rather low-key. Yet somehow, the product was more powerful because it wasn't as complete as a video stream of the event. Like a knowledge asset, the added value came through the accessibility and extraction of key points. Interestingly, several years later, the Web site is still accessed – dipped into for key quotes and summaries, whereas the VHS videos have been all but discarded. We felt that we had discovered something powerful in having a near real-time abridged summary of the event, complete with photographs, audio clips and a simple process for anyone, anywhere in the company to participate in the discussion.

In the years that have passed since the Innovation Colloquium, information technology has advanced, and many variations and adaptations of this approach have been tried and tested in BP.

Several workshops and events have been recorded onto CD-ROM, and distributed to a wider audience. This medium enables far greater use of video than the company intranet would support, in effect converting each event into an electronic learning tool.

Typically, such tools would include:

- a simple, easily navigable index of the event;

- succinct video clips of speakers synchronized with their presentation material – often PowerPoint slides;

- longer videos to add further depth to the succinct sound bites if the reader requires it;

- full, searchable transcript of everything that was said on the videos;

- copies of all the presentation materials used;

- videos of the attendees expressing their impressions of the event; and

- contact information for all the attendees.

News media and broadcasting companies are past masters at the packaging of captured knowledge as powerful, educational knowledge assets.

The accompanying CD includes a link to one of the best examples that we have found – the BBC's 'The AIDS Debate' contains a mix of features, personal stories, quotes, key facts, links to experts, quizzes, recorded 'chat sessions' video clips and audio recordings – all presented in an easily navigable portal format.

It makes most corporate intranets seem lightweight by comparison. Why not use it to inspire the intranet manager in your organization?

Capturing knowledge from someone leaving their position

Ideally, if knowledge management principles have been applied during the time an employee spends with the company, then much of that person's knowledge will have been captured over time in e-mails, discussion forums and knowledge assets. Knowledge capture and transfer is a natural outcome of all of the processes and tools referenced in this book, hence personal knowledge capture should not be the only record of an individual's contribution to the company.

Here's an example of this.

When the majority of BP's knowledge management team left the company in 1999, a huge amount of their personal knowledge and experience was already embedded in a rich Web site (effectively a knowledge asset), an extensive discussion forum, and a community of several hundred enthusiasts remaining in the company. Writing this book would have been a far greater challenge without the commitment of the team to live their own principles.

If you're already managing knowledge routinely, then the personal loss is diminished

However, we recognize that the real world doesn't always operate as smoothly as an elegant model ...

Retaining corporate memory when people move on

Think about the last time that you moved on from a position. Did you capture anything for the person filling your role? Or think about when you started your current role. What questions would you have liked your predecessor to answer?

At times of significant business restructuring, many people will be leaving their jobs, either to move somewhere else in the organization, or to leave the company completely. In day-to-day business, people move rapidly from one field to another unrelated position elsewhere in the company. Very often these people possess key knowledge – knowledge either about the business and their role, or about a discipline or function.

What about the 'what's in it for me' factor? Why should someone actually want to capture their personal knowledge?

Leavers who have had the opportunity to talk through their job, feel better about leaving (even if they are leaving the company involuntarily). They feel a sense of closure, and they feel a sense of professional satisfaction that they are leaving the post, or the community, in safe hands.

How can we retain knowledge when the people move on? It would be wonderful to say that we use these techniques with every member of staff leaving the company but the truth is that we're not particularly good at this. Where this approach to personal knowledge capture *has* been effective in BP, the six steps below illustrate what was done.

Find a customer (or customers) for the knowledge

Who needs to know what the leaver knows? In the case of a key business player, it may well be his/her successor who is the customer for the knowledge. It the leaver is a global expert, then the customer for the knowledge is a network, or someone acting on behalf of the network.

Facilitator's notes: What if no successor has been identified yet? In this case it is perhaps even more important that someone takes responsibility for capturing the knowledge, so the successor can be briefed when he/she is appointed.

Six steps for successful knowledge capture from an individual

1 Find out what knowledge needs to be transferred

Just like the guidelines for building a knowledge asset earlier in the chapter, the first step is to identify the 'customer'. Having done this, you will need to strike a balance between 'What does the customer want to know about?' and 'What knowledge does the leaver feel is crucial?'

Balancing what needs to be heard with what needs to be said

There are two basic approaches to deciding what knowledge needs to be transferred.

Firstly you can ask the leaver to identify the key knowledge, and this is best done using a checklist of questions designed to make him or her think carefully about what they know.

Facilitator's notes: The purpose of the checklist is to get at the things which the leaver does not necessarily realize they know - those bits of knowledge which are automatic or subconscious, but crucial to the job. At this stage the leaver is not trying to capture the knowledge itself, but to identify the priority areas. The second approach is to ask what knowledge the customer wants to gain.

Chris Dewey leads a network of 50 worldwide professionals concerned with knowledge about grease, and was planning to capture knowledge from a global expert in the subject of grease lubricants. She went out to the Grease network and asked them each for three questions they would like the expert to answer. Many of them came back and said that three was not enough - they had dozens of questions!

By asking for three, or five, or ten questions and comparing the knowledge needs of the customer and the 'knowledge offers' from the leaver, you can then build a list of prioritized knowledge areas that need to be transferred.

2 Develop a plan to capture and transfer the knowledge

Now you know which are the key areas of knowledge which need to be retained when the leaver moves on. How do you most effectively capture it and transfer it?

The answer to this depends very much on whether it is a job handover, where someone will be filling the leaver's post. If this is the case, then the best plan is to set up a meeting or meetings between the leaver and his/her successor. You can then give the successor accountability for capturing all the knowledge they think they might need. In certain circumstances, where there are other customers for the knowledge in addition to the successor, you might like to include some of these people in the meeting.

If there is no clear successor, or (as in the case of a global expert leaving) the knowledge is needed by a whole community of people, then alternative approaches are needed.

Although the leaver could try to capture all the knowledge themselves, it is better to do it with a facilitator, or an interviewer, or (best of all) a representative of the network or community. If you are able to schedule and record a live Web-chat with the community, this can create a powerful record, as the different community members will build-off one another's questions. The

BBC's 'The AIDS Debate' example mentioned earlier includes examples of recorded Web-chats.

3 Conduct the interview

It's a good idea to go through the knowledge transfer meetings using some sort of checklist or structure, so that all areas of knowledge transfer are covered.

Not just know-how – but know-what, know-why and know-who as well!

Rather than just concentrating on 'know-how', consider 'know-who', 'know-what', and 'know-why'. Use prompts to jog the leaver's memory, as described below. Tape-record, or even video the meeting so that you can produce a transcript, and some useful sound bites. This will be a very rich experience, and you may not get a second chance.

Facilitator's notes: Remember, this is intended to be a mutually beneficial conversation rather than an audit or inquisition. Be sensitive at all times to what the leaver is comfortable discussing.

4 Publish this 'personal knowledge asset'

If the knowledge only needs to pass from the leaver to the successor, then you don't need to do much 'packaging'. The successor can keep it all on file somewhere, or in written notes and transcripts. If the knowledge needs to go to a network, or community of practice, then more effort is needed. This knowledge will need to be made accessible and searchable to the whole network, which probably means putting it on the intranet. Some of the ideas you could consider are as follows:

- Writing a frequently asked questions (FAQ) based on the questions from the network and the expert's answers, and make it widely available.

- Using the expert's presentations, plus his recorded comments on each slide, as a teaching aid.

- Copying the title page of each of his/her books, and recording a paragraph of his comments on each one.

- Recording video summaries of key issues.

- Summarizing his/her key stories, to act as company history.

- Summarizing his/her recommendations, illustrated by key quotes, to act as the basis for a knowledge asset.

- Creating a 'relationship map' of key contacts, complete with photographs.

What you should have at this stage is a set of captured knowledge (in the form of notes, a Web site, video, or transcribed tapes), a successor or customer group who feel they have been briefed, and a happy leaver with a sense that they are valued.

5 Stay in touch

Don't cut the cords – stay connected

Just as is the case for a knowledge asset, links to people are a critical component. Aim to stay in touch with the leaver if you possibly can. No knowledge transfer or capture will ever be 100 per cent, and there will come a time when you think of that key question you wish you had asked. Make sure you can contact the leaver in future so you can tap his/her experience again. Your company may have invested heavily in developing this individual – you will know of their professional quality and they will know about the company culture. You may want to bring them back on a consultancy basis in the future. BP's yellow-pages directory (see Chapter 10, Finding the Right People – If Only I Knew Who), 'Connect' includes the capacity for staff leaving the company to leave their details 'in the system' after they have left the company, if they choose to.

6 Summary

We have now considered three approaches to capturing knowledge – consolidating a set of stories into a community-owned knowledge asset, capturing an event, and retaining corporate memory by interviewing a member of staff about to leave their current role. Knowledge capture in any form takes time and effort, but the potential yield to BP and other organizations has been high – millions of dollars in some cases, so the time and effort is well spent.

Capturing knowledge is a powerful way to share what has been learned, but you need to find a way to extract the learning first. This chapter will be put into perspective when read with Chapters 7, 8 and, particularly, Chapter 9 – Learning After Doing – When It's All Over.

Part III
Today and Tomorrow

In the previous chapters we have shared the tools and methods that we applied within BP to practice knowledge management. This chapter presumes knowledge of the other chapters; so if you started here, skip back to the earlier chapters. So, where do we go next? What is the 'next wave' for knowledge management? This chapter is about how we are developing the capability in the organization to manage knowledge without help from a central resource – allowing us to move on to other challenges.

The chapter includes:

• Preparing to let go.

• The phases of knowledge management activity.

• Working yourself out of a job.

• Focusing on a company-wide business process.

• Where next?

Learning to fly

magine an eagle encouraging its young to leave the nest. They huddle together in the nest, high up on a wild crag. When the mist lifts they can see forever. The parents have nurtured them, sheltered them from the wind and rain and protected them from prey. Now it is time for them to fly. There is no way for them to clamber down the cliff and practice on the beginners' slopes! So the mother pushes them out of the nest with her beak and watches anxiously.

Down, down, down they drop. Their wings come out to steady them. Their feet reach out towards the ground as if to push themselves back, and their beaks reach upward. Still they drop. They continuously beat their wings. The ground is fast approaching. Slowly they pull out of the hurtling drop and glide over the treetops. They beat their wings some more, more assured this time. Without looking back they head across the lakeshore looking to fend for themselves.

In time the mother catches up with them and demonstrates the art of catching a warm thermal current, to elevate themselves to a higher level. They glide along the face of the crags, looking graceful and powerful. In fact they look as if they have been flying forever.

In time they will mate and have offspring. They too will have to stand back and let others learn to fly.

Engagement

We also have to learn to stand back and let others learn to do it for themselves. Sometimes we are anxious. Based on our experience of applying knowledge management techniques we see some distinct stages in the relationship between a central KM resource and the business teams that they work with.

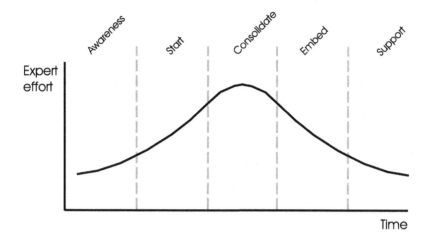

Creating *awareness*. This involves a presen- Awareness
tation and discussion about what knowledge
management is and where it has been used to
leverage business results. Examples of successful application
are key to enrolling others. This is most powerful if peers speak
about how they have applied knowledge management, and the
difference that it has made to their business. A practical way
we have found to do this, if the peer is in a different location,
is to record and show a short video clip. The awareness stage is
a two-way exchange. What is the biggest current issue or challenge for the business team?

Starting with something simple. Applying one of Start with something
the tools and techniques in this book to address simple
a simple part of the issue is a good start. Demonstrating a 'quick win' is important to gain
the interest and commitment of the team. If they see these
techniques can be applied – to deliver some tangible results
without spending too much time on them – then they are likely
to come back for more. We have found it best to introduce some
formality after this stage into the planning. What specifically will
be done, what are the costs and the benefits and will the team
commit some resources to it?

Consolidate using the holistic model

Consolidate. This builds on the simple beginning using the holistic model. Exactly what is done depends on the nature of the business challenge, on existing strengths and on priorities for learning. It is likely the team will need some expert resource working directly with them, and at the same time they should encourage widening the number of people exposed to the processes.

Embed in business processes

Embed. At this stage the business team takes the lead and links what they are doing to their routine business processes. Meanwhile the experts take the role of advisors, and introduce new tools where appropriate.

Support. The experts have moved out from amongst the business team, but are available by telephone, e-mail and videoconference to encourage and support the efforts of the business. They also connect the business to others who could help or benefit from the learning.

The toughest part is letting go

In working through this sequence a number of times, we always find that the toughest part is letting go. The business teams are busy and are grateful for the contribution from the experts. It takes the pressure off them, and they are helping deliver the business objectives. It creates a dependency relationship. The experts feel good that they are needed. However, if the benefits are to be sustainable then the team must solve problems on their own. This will free the central resource to move on to the next task, building on what has been learned from this one.

In some ways I suppose it's the same as letting go of teenage children. My two have grown up. I am not quite sure when it happened. I used to make all the decisions for them, but now they have minds of their own. My son drives the family car late at night and we worry till he is back. My daughter goes out clubbing and catches a taxi back in the early hours. Will she be safe? We have shared our values and behaviours with our children for several years. They have watched what we do as much as what we say. We have instilled in them a capability to survive. Now they must take their own decisions. And we must learn to let go. If they want advice from us they'll ask for it.

So, as a central KM team we have instilled in the organization the capacity to share and apply know-how. The team has disbanded. Some have found new challenges within the company where they can make a significant difference. Others have left to consult externally. In either case, as external or internal consultants, success in embedding knowledge management in one project is the reference required for getting the next job.

> Learning to live without a central knowledge-management resource

Let's stop and reflect for a moment. Identify three areas of your organization or department where you can make the biggest difference to performance. Then look at the holistic model to use as a check (see below, and also Chapter 3, The Holistic Model). Are you learning before, during and after? Do you have a way for routinely capturing and refreshing the knowledge gained? Who are the people are involved? Is there a community who feel accountable for looking after and sustaining this knowledge?

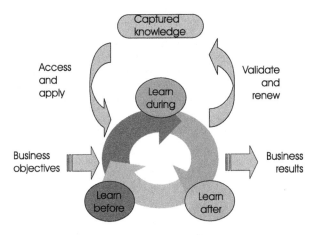

| Embedding knowledge management in core processes | BP has some key company-wide processes: health, safety and environmental (HSE) performance; capital productivity; and operational excellence. KM principles are being embedded in each of these so that they become the normal |

way of doing business. If we can share a good practice from one business and replicate it in several other places just think of the potential value added. The aim is to improve collaboration, the role of networks as guardians of the company's knowledge, recognizing and using the value of the company's knowledge and reducing the time to competency by linking knowledge assets to the learning programme. These are the 'thermals' that will sustain the young bird in flight, and enable it to soar higher.

Let's have a look at what is happening.

Knowledge management and HSE performance

| No harm to people or the environment | Health, safety and environmental performance is high profile across the entire company. It is something that every employee is accountable for, and something that is actively promoted in all offices (remember those stickers on the |

mirrors in the earlier chapter?). This is one area where every business is truly committed to improve so as not to harm people or the environment.

So how is knowledge management embedded into the HSE programme?

BP's policy on health, safety and the environment makes no mention of knowledge management. However it does explicitly reference *learning*:

'*How we learn from each other ...*

'*The HSE Toolbox will be maintained on the intranet containing good operating processes/practices, knowledge and audit protocols. These show good demonstrated practice from around the BP Group, and should be referenced when developing business management systems. More importantly, business personnel are encouraged to contribute their good practices to the HSE Toolbox in order to promote sharing and adoption of lessons learned.'*

There is an HSE Web site that provides a focal point for all issues to do with health, safety and the environment. There is an assessment tool that enables different sites to check how their performance is and what they might do to improve.

An intranet-based 'HSE Toolbox' is available to all staff, and provides details on good practices, assigned to the various HSE management processes. Networks of staff take responsibility for each management process, and act as owners for the good practices in that area. This shared approach ensures a flow of new good practices, refreshing what is held in the toolbox. The whole process operates in a similar manner to the way we create and maintain knowledge assets (see Chapter 12 for more on capturing knowledge) – but we don't refer to knowledge assets anywhere – we simply call it a 'toolbox'.

> Knowledge assets under a different guise

Whilst BP puts tremendous effort into avoiding health, safety or environmentally-related incidents, any incident or near miss is captured as part of a reporting system. The lessons learned from the incident are drawn out as part of the reporting process, and shared widely and rapidly across the organization.

A network of HSE staff around the company feels accountable for improving against their performance targets, and so maintains the knowledge and shares it quickly around the organization.

Knowledge management and projects

Company-wide, BP invests billions of dollars in projects each year: searching for new reserves of oil, accessing new markets for new products, building factories for the construction of solar cells, researching and developing cleaner fuels ...

Are we doing the right projects?

Much management attention is devoted to improving the productivity of our capital projects, asking questions such as:

- How do we know that we are doing the *right* project?

- How do we know that we're doing the project *right*?

- What are the key risks associated with this project?

- How does our return on investment compare with industry benchmarks?

Whether your projects have a budget of £10,000 or £100,000,000 you'll want to ensure that each project is managed in way that builds in the lessons and insights from other projects. But how can you create the impetus for learning, when project teams have a natural instinct to get into action?

BP's process for managing the life cycle of a project is known as the capital value process (CVP). It provides a framework for any project team, with a series of recognizable phases, and stage-gates that represent the decision points in moving ahead with the next stage of a project, a chance to pause and reflect before committing the next tranche of money.

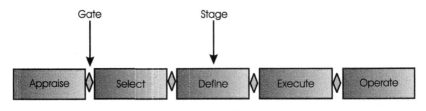

Capital value process – 5 stages

This process is used across the company, and has created a common language across project teams. When a team running a project to build retail sites in Poland talks with a team producing oil from the depths of the Gulf of Mexico, a common understanding that they are both working in the 'define' stage of their respective projects will help them better understand each other's challenges.

... And are we doing them right?

So how is knowledge management used in this process?

For some time, a community of project-management professionals has been disciplined at holding post-project appraisals to capture the lessons from major projects. BP has been putting effort into energizing this community, to get them acting as the guardians of the community's knowledge, and for refreshing and keeping the know-how alive. A synthesis of these good practices is embedded in value improvement processes recognized by the projects community as a whole.

The CVP framework for managing projects includes some mandatory elements - things that a project team *must* do, in order to gain sanction for the next stage of a project. One of the necessary tasks to be completed for every stage is that the team hold a peer assist meeting (see Chapter 7 for more on peer assists), which gets creative input and options into their work, and a peer review, which is a way to get constructive challenge from other peer teams.

The impact of this simple, common process is very strong. Nobody can complete a project without learning from his or her peers on several occasions, and without seeking out which good practices can be applied from others.

Perhaps you are reading this thinking 'that's all very well, but we could never make such a rigorous process work in our company'. Or perhaps 'our projects are much smaller scale, there is too much additional overhead in a process like this'.

The power of a management team 'asking the right questions'

If embedding prompts for learning and knowledge-sharing into a process is not feasible, another option is to embed it into management behaviour by encouraging management to ask questions such as:

- Who has done this kind of thing before, that we can learn from?

- Who did you learn from before coming to me with this new idea?

- Who might benefit from knowing about what you've just achieved?

BP's Cooper River chemical factory in Texas did exactly this, and it quickly evolved into a low-key, but highly effective initiative they entitled 'borrowing and sharing'. A member of their administrative staff, maintains a register of good practices that anyone at the factory has imported and applied (with measures of value where possible), or has been exported and applied by another business. Each year Cooper River's management team set an annual target for the number of good practices imported and exported (set at 70 at the time of writing).

Knowledge management is the lazy man's way to work!

This simple act of *asking the right management questions* and keeping a register to raise the profile, has created a positive learning culture at the factory, which one of the workers referred to, in a tongue-in-cheek manner, as 'the lazy man's way to work'. That's certainly an interesting way to paraphrase 'knowledge management'!

And finally let's look at the role of knowledge management in the area of operations.

Knowledge management and operations excellence

We're going to spend a bit of time on this one, describing how we have put it all together. We have created a community of practice across all of our operational businesses, providing tools, processes and encouraging the right behaviours to 'harness the knowledge of a thousand control rooms'.

BP has a flat organizational structure – around 150 businesses – in what we describe as a 'federation of assets'. Two thirds of these business units are directly involved in operations of some description, hence there is high potential for

> Encouraging sharing in a flat organization

sharing knowledge. Each asset operates with a high degree of autonomy, functioning almost as a discrete company, highly focused on performance.

One risk that a flat organizational structure carries is that the businesses operate independently, rather than interdependently, with the consequence that we don't capture the synergies and economies of scale. Business leaders were incentivised to help each other by getting a portion of their remuneration for the total results not just their own business results. The operations excellence initiative was established to encourage sharing, not only between businesses of similar type (refineries, or manufacturing operations for example), but also across operations of different character. Underpinning this was a belief that the key processes of managing operations are actually common, regardless of whether the business is an offshore platform producing oil, or a factory producing polyethylene in Asia.

All of our operations people are working with issues relating to:

- the management of people;

- safety and environmental performance;

- the ability to minimize unplanned down-time;

- effective project management;

- ensuring optimal production; and

- rigorous cost management.

Check with the holistic model

So let's refer again to the holistic model for a moment (see the figure on p. 265).

Are we focused on delivering business results? Yes! So what are we doing to ensure learning before, during and after? What network is in place to facilitate the sharing? And what are we doing to continually capture the latest knowledge?

Common measures and a common assessment tool

Having recognized that our various operating businesses had more in common with each other than they might have thought, the next stage was to create a common language, a standard set of measures, and a single assessment tool, which could be used universally to gauge performance and provide assurance for management.

Creating a common language is a basis for sharing

A diverse team of operations staff representative of all our operating environments came together for several days to establish a common set of practices. Examples of these practices include: raising morale and motivation, managing energy efficiency, forecasting production, and managing greenhouse gas emissions.

The full list of 25 practices is included as Appendix B.

The team designed a five-level assessment tool as described in Chapter 6. The assessment tool was offered to all one hundred operating businesses for them to assess their own strengths and areas for improvement. Typically the operations manager would draw together a group of ten to twenty people – a diagonal slice through their organization – and the group would discuss and agree which of the statements was true from their perspective. This would provide an overall score for each practice – *'We are level three for managing greenhouse gases'* – for example. Often the individuals would disagree. In their experience the business was more or less competent in that practice. By giving an example the group could identify times when they were performing more competently.

In addition to stating their current position, the team were encouraged to prioritize three practices to improve during the next year. *'We are currently level three for managing greenhouse gases, and have set a target to be at level five by end 2002'* would be an example of this.

So that was it. Every operating business works through the self-assessment and records two sets of scores – where they are today, and where they plan to be in a year's time. We captured these scores via an intranet Web site. Having identified some gaps in their performance, the business would agree some specific actions relating to closing these gaps, and spend the remainder of the year actively working towards those targets.

Providing the tools and resources that support improvement

Having a common set of practices enabled us to create a 'toolbox' (much like the earlier HSE example) of good practices, tips and techniques, each one allied to a particular practice. We built in a feature similar to one in Amazon.com that enables anyone to review an entry in the toolbox, and provide a 'star rating' from one to five. This democratic approach helped us to see which tools were truly useful.

> The community maintains and refreshes its tools

Additionally, we worked to align a network with each of the practices, such that the network would become accountable for the range of tools and good practices available for that particular practice. In some cases this required us to merge several networks into one, whilst in others a new network was encouraged to form.

In this way, the toolbox acted as a collection of knowledge assets that enable learning from what the company already knows, whether before, during or after an operational phase (see Chapter 12 for more on knowledge assets). BP's various operations networks became the custodians for each one, renewing and updating it based on the star ratings provided by those actually using the tools.

Having a *common* set of assessment measures across all of our hundred business operations enabled us to create a river diagram (see Chapter 6. p. 85). The picture portrays the range of scores against all of the practice areas that we had defined, and can be used as a backdrop against which any single business could measure itself. The river diagram proved to be a popular way to think about performance relative to the company as a whole. It tells an operations manager how strong or weak their perform- ance was relative to all others. By referring to the picture the whole team could see the areas it performed well in, and areas where others were better. This is the first step towards asking for and receiving help. Having a common language and a common self-assessment tool for all operations is tremendously powerful, and enables sharing between previously unrelated businesses.

Because we had divided the assessment tool into practices, we measured the scores for each practice. We consciously declined to sum the scores across the practices to get an absolute score for a refinery or a chemical factory. We weren't interested in absolute comparison – we wanted to share the details on a prac- tice-by-practice basis. Because *everyone* has something to share and *everyone* has something to learn.

In summary, what could have been a simple league table of performance which drove defensive and competitive behaviours into the company actually became a vehicle for knowledge sharing which acknowledged strengths, and encouraged others to seek out help. There were some peer challenges to the relative positions of different businesses and that was healthy. After all the scores are only self-perceptions and led to a dialogue as to what was good practice.

> Everyone has something to share and everyone has something to learn.

'If I'm at level 3, who can I talk to who is at level 4 or 5?' The stairs diagrams in Chapter 6 p. 88) were an easy way to determine who to learn from. Usually it wasn't a one-to-one exchange, but everyone with a desire to learn met with several people with strength in that practice to share experience. The flow of knowledge was rarely one way and everyone went away with concrete actions to improve their competence.

These exchanges of experience and knowledge are run as peer assist meetings, or workshops, to discuss areas of common interest. One example of this was a workshop on the subject of reliability at a high performing refinery in Castellon, Spain. Representatives from a high-performing chemicals factory and an upstream production platform, joined Castellon along with staff from different businesses that wanted to improve their reliability. There was some reluctance to participate. People doubted they could learn from a very different business to their own. Within 30 minutes participants were in animated conversation, realizing they had similar problems and were talking a common language. The conversation did not let up for two days till it was time to return to their own sites. Every one left with ideas of how to improve reliability - even the high performing sites. The event was captured on video and synthesized into generic advice, backed up by the voice of experience on a CD-ROM-based knowledge asset for wider use.

Offers and requests – lessons from the nudist beach!

Asking for help – an unnatural act?

I can't confess to have any naturist tendencies whatsoever. The idea of taking off all my clothes on a public beach... well, call me a prude, but it's decidedly un-natural for me!

However, if I absolutely *had to,* I suppose I'd rather go naked on a nudist beach than anywhere else – at least I would be in an environment where taking clothes off was the norm ...

One consequence of our macho 'engineering culture' is that *asking for help* is unnatural. Some people feel vulnerable when they admit that they could benefit from the experience of others; consequently, asking for help can feel like a show of weakness.

In designing the operations excellence process, we recognized this aspect of our culture and set out to create the organizational equivalent of a nudist beach for macho operations managers who needed help. Now that *is* frightening imagery – let's move swiftly on!

Here's what we did. As part of the process, after completion of the assessment we added one final stage. Every business was encouraged to make 'three offers and three requests'. An 'offer' in this context is an offer of expertise or help, based on a particular strength, complete with individual contact names and details.

Some examples:

> *'Within Canada Gas we have every employee involved in community activities within the regions we operate. We have an excellent reputation and are happy to share the ways in which we have set up these relationships.'*

> *'Pasadena has extensive experience in the area of managing contract and third party staff, as a result of the plant/business*

acquisition in 1996. We have a lot of lessons-learned to share regarding contract working, relationship management, and cost control. Note that these lessons-learned encompass both good and not-so-good experiences!'

'Texas City's offer: over the last two years have significantly improved safety performance. We offer to share experience of two main initiatives - advanced safety auditing and site wide communication.'

A 'request' is a specific appeal for assistance – for example:

'Our Pipeline System spans some 150 kilometres onshore and involves several distinct assets. We generally need to improve shift handover routines and basic communication within our organization and between sites. We'd welcome some new ideas on good handover/communication techniques. What do you do that's different?'
'We often end up losing more production than originally planned during shutdowns, mainly because of problems on restart, (We deliver shutdown within the planned time-frame but take longer than planned to get back to full stable production). Often the problems that caused the delayed return to full production are to do with parts of the plant we didn't touch during the shutdown. We would like to learn from others who have overcome these problems.'
'We request examples of processes used to maintain morale and motivation in a very challenging business environment where the site performance must improve significantly very quickly.'

By institutionalizing this exchange of offers and requests into the overall process, we defused the awkwardness of asking for help, and the self-conscious modesty that might prevent businesses feeling that they had anything to contribute. 'Everyone is doing it, so what are your three offers and requests?'

> Making offers and requests

A community Web site

A community centre

To create a sense of community, we commissioned a smart Web-based environment to support the exchange of good practices, offers and requests throughout the operations community of 30,000 staff.

Through this, we have provided an electronic environment where any of our operations staff can:

- publish news items, upcoming events of interest and success stories into a shared 'newspaper';

- participate in discussion forums on technical subjects;

- view all the offers and requests made to date;

- discover who else was connected to the Web site at that moment in time and initiate a chat session with them;

- conduct the assessment online, generating a customized 'river diagram' for their business in real-time; and

- discover tools to help improve performance in a specific practice, and provide a review of that tool in a similar manner to the book reviews on Amazon.com.

This Web-based 'community space' is hosted by a full-time operations professional, based at a refinery. He acts as a focal point for this huge community of operators around the world, making introductions and connections, canvassing them for successes, initiating conversations, chats and discussion threads.

Capturing the knowledge

Knowledge has built up along with the communities that use and nurture it. We have CD-ROMs which contain the distilled good practices and also video clips of people who may help.

Building knowledge and community together

On the community Web site we have a store of useful tools, documents, good practices etc. We have identified the knowledge gaps through the assessment and river diagram. These are areas in which the company needs to learn more. Action plans are in hand to address these.

In summary, what have we achieved with operations excellence? In creating this process we did not consciously use the holistic model except for an occasional review of what else we might do. We had reached the stage of unconscious competence.

- We introduced a new company-wide process based on the creation of a common language, a standard set of measures and a common assessment.

- We created some new ways to visualize overall performance, linking together good performers with those actively seeking improvement.

- We overcame the natural reluctance to ask for help by encouraging the sharing of offers and requests across the company.

- We created a community that was committed to help each other improve.

- We supported all of the above with enabling technology, and identified a new role for one of our operations supervisors.

And we achieved this without mentioning the words 'knowledge management' to anyone!

So that's three areas we have found to embed our KM principles. Today there are many more examples within BP, both technical and non technical. We have moved on to apply these principles in different settings, in very different organizations. The principles are robust and we are still learning a lot!

Have a think: 'Where are the knowledge gaps for your organization – the ones that if plugged would add significant value?' And then figure out how you can use some of the tools and techniques described earlier in this book to embed them in your business processes.

Of course this process of awareness, starting, consolidating, embedding and supporting is not linear, it is a life cycle. As an organization develops, expanding and contracting, acquiring and divesting - then it is necessary to check where you are in the life cycle and put effort in accordingly. You cannot relax. The job is never complete. There is no room for complacency. The bringing together of two or more companies brings its own challenges - of different culture and language, separate networks, and different practices, but to capture the synergies it is necessary to acknowledge the differences and learn from them; to learn why the different contexts led to different experiences, language and practices.

And that's where the fun starts again! There are always benefits in the diversity but the 'way we do things' is hard to let go!

What was supposed to happen?

We set out to write a book and tell you about knowledge management; to capture and display for you a vivid picture of what we have learned about managing knowledge in BP over the past five years. We have received, and continue to get, lots of requests about how we 'do' knowledge management inside BP. We have read others' perceptions of what BP does, and we wanted to record our own story of what goes on inside BP and how knowledge management is evolving.

We wanted it to be a practical book; you can read it and instantly do something with your knowledge. We perceived it would fill a gap. It would be readily snapped up in airport bookshops and in business school libraries.

We wanted to acknowledge the contribution to collective learning, of the KM team, and of the varied practitioners throughout our organization.

What actually happened?

The idea was first articulated on a long transatlantic flight. It's amazing how the reduced oxygen at 35,000 feet makes one so much more creative!

We researched how to write a book. We read one about the topic, we searched the Internet for experiences and we spoke to people who had succeeded. We considered the options. Could we publish it ourselves? Do we need an agent? Where are the gaps in the market? Is there a market? We did some research, but we didn't overdo it.

We got clear on what the book would be about; we worked out the principles and the tools to include. Then we sketched out what needed to go into a proposal. We created the market in our mind.

We chose a chapter each, one for which we knew the subject well and started writing. We swapped chapters and amended each other's. It was a real test of how well we, having very different styles of working, could work together.

We had several publishers interested; we selected one we could work with. Our criteria for selection changed. We went for one that believed in the subject we were writing about and one that had fresh ideas.

We had lots of informal reviews. After editing each other's chapters we agreed common approaches before writing the next. We found ourselves looking at books through different lenses. It gave us ideas about which books work and which don't.

We agreed which chapters we would write individually; we worked on those in which we had most interest and most experience. The rest we wrote together.

We put the pages up on the wall, sorted by chapter; in effect we created our own 'War room'. We spotted that the first few chapters set the context and model, and the next set are the tools and techniques. Amazingly we hadn't spotted that distinction before!

As we finished a chapter we sent it to the publisher and requested feedback so that we could build that learning into what we wrote next. They challenged us to include a wider range of stories, beyond BP. We realized we wanted to use stories within our own experience, within BP, but we wanted to find a way to make it relevant to people in smaller organizations. We did that by telling stories and by asking questions to get the reader to reflect. Well, did we?

The book came together faster than we expected. The story was easy to tell. We had estimated the time we were prepared to spend on it and estimated the number of words per chapter. We worked best writing with the flow, then editing it afterwards. Collecting the information together then arranging it proved to be clumsy.

We have written a book that describes the fruits of our own experiences in the same way that we might tell a colleague. Knowledge management is a simple idea. The hard bit is in the doing.

What was different between what happened and what was meant to happen?

We delivered ahead of plan, partly because we kept each other honest, and partly because the birth of Hannah was there as a milestone. We thought it would require more in terms of sacrifice of time at home.

We said we would create Internet-style pages. In fact we have created a knowledge asset. It is consistent with our model. In writing this book we have lived and breathed the principles we espouse.

We made explicit the division between the first half about a model and a context for knowledge management and second half about tools for knowledge management.

We found writing enjoyable rather than a chore, there was something missing when we got to the end.

What have we learned?

We have learned that we can step outside of our area of expertise (neither of us has written a book before) and use the principles of knowledge management to get very quickly up the learning curve.

The exercise has proved to be a good health check on where we are with knowledge management in BP. We found what was truly sustainable within the company. The act of writing it down helped clarify our learning; we have converted tacit to explicit.

'Having read that chapter I finally got it.'

It has made us realize that we have made some progress but there is much more to do.

We learned once again that people are important. The relationship with the publisher is important. We made direct requests of people and were never refused. We asked other authors for advice, we asked for endorsements, for quotes, for review. People were always supportive and constructive.

We learned that the driving force for writing the book was wanting to tell the story our way, not making money, nor building our reputation.

We learned to complement each other's different styles until we could finish each other's sentences!

Chris Collison and Geoff Parcell, September 2000

Looking back over nearly four years – a brief retrospect

What did we set out to do?

In writing the second edition we want to show the viral effect of knowledge management, how the tools have been applied and adapted to many different contexts, and how the overall body of knowledge in the book could be built up by broadening the story to embrace many other organizations.

What did we achieve?

We've just reached sales of 10,000 with the first edition. It has been translated into Spanish, Mandarin Chinese and Slovenian. The book has received many positive reviews. We have a lively discussion forum with 500 people, a self-helping community. We have helped people inside and outside BP to make KM work for them.

What went well? Why?

We like the style of the book and have grown fond of the cover design. 10,000 copies have been sold and even more people have read it.

With this book we walked the talk. We shared a knowledge asset on KM. We have now captured readers' experiences to add to and enrich that knowledge asset.

We found that knowledge management networks, discussion groups and journals were effective channels. Identifying the 'connectors' in these networks (people like Denham Grey, David Skyrme and Dave Gurteen) and asking them for their opinion on the book and how to develop its market, proved to be a successful strategy. People really do want to help!

Publishing the book enhanced our reputation; it provided us with a springboard to do other things. It has given us an opportunity to use the contents of the book in other settings - Chris in Centrica and Geoff in the United Nations. It has heightened our awareness of what else contributes to creating a sharing and learning environment. Above all it has given us the chance to continue learning.

Many people gratefully tell us they have used the techniques and they have made a big difference very quickly. Frequently we hear 'I've given my copy away - I'll have to get another.' Or 'I haven't read it yet but my wife has.' The development sector - NGOs and UN agencies particularly - appreciate and are using the techniques.

We found that the self-assessment approach and the river diagram were highly transferable, and created new entry points for knowledge management. We were so struck by the power of these techniques that we restructured the book to add a new chapter.

The 'Learning to Fly' community responded positively and creatively when we asked them for their ideas for the new edition, and their contributions as stories. This book wouldn't have happened without them.

Writing the second edition with Geoff in Geneva and Chris in Windsor went surprisingly well. Having developed the ability to finish each others' sentences during our time together in BP, we put that same trust and understanding into practice through a series of e-mails and phone calls. We still needed to get together to lay out the book in its entirety and check for consistency - which became a fantastic excuse for a memorable long weekend with the family in Geneva!

What could have gone better? Why?

Marketing. It is still not in airport bookshops as we had hoped.

We haven't yet made it into *Management Today* or *The Economist*. Amazon is our biggest outlet. It has the potential to be a general business book, rather than a book for KM specialists. KM is everyone's business.

We need to get better at aligning the marketing to our own conference and meeting schedule. This will enable the book to be accessible to people when they have an interest in it.

We wanted to make the book like a Web site. By adding a CD to the second edition this makes it more so. We can provide access to resources related to specific chapters. Now if we could only hyperlink from the printed page ...

Marks out of ten?

Eight. What would have made it ten? If sales had reached 25,000 already. If we saw it in airport bookshops. If we saw people reading it in public places. If it was on the core curriculum of most MBA courses, rather than a few. If it was a place where people could add their own experiences automatically ...

Chris Collison and Geoff Parcell, June 2004

Footnote

Incidentally in case you are still curious, BP has made the project work in Vietnam, producing gas offshore in the Nam Con Son basin, piping it ashore, processing it, converting it to electricity to supply the major cities of Vietnam to help their industry grow.

And I did get that kitchen finished, and we are proud to invite our dinner guests into the kitchen, sometimes we don't quite move out! But we've never cooked the television presenter's favourite dish, Coquilles St. Jacques with mange tout and fried potato wafers.

Appendix A
– Storyboard

In pulling together feedback for a peer assist it is good to let the whole team of visitors work together on the feedback. If it is left to one or two to construct the presentation then often the feedback loses some of its richness. We have found the storyboarding technique useful if involving everybody in creating the story.

Usually we work around a flipchart to focus everyone on the same page.

The first thing to agree on is the purpose of the presentation or feedback. In the case of a peer assist it is usually to highlight what has been done well and some options and insights for improving the final activity or project.

Agree the purpose

Identify the three key messages you want your audience to leave with. By limiting it to only three will demand some discussion of priorities and what will really make the difference. By focussing on the messages you want the audience to leave with ensures you give some thought to how your feedback lands rather than just what you want to tell them. For instance if you say 'Here are two areas where you didn't involve the right people', the message received might be 'they think we should have asked for their opinion earlier'.

Identify the three key messages

Having identified the three key messages divide a flipchart page into eight equal frames. In the first one write 'Intro and Purpose' and in the last one write 'three key messages'.

1 Intro+ Purpose	5
2	6
3	7
4	8 3 Key messages

Note the three points to make

Take the first key message. What are the important points to get across? Draw a picture and the three or four associated points.

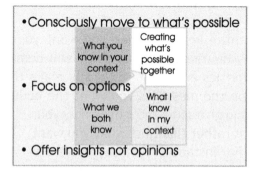

Use between one and three frames to address each message. Once you have finished, look through the flow. What have you missed? Would it be better if you reordered it? If you were receiving this feedback how would it land? Would you walk away with the desired three key messages?

Here's an example of a storyboard for explaining the peer assist process.

Action **Purpose:** To share my understanding of the peer assist process	• Avoid the 'usual suspects' • 6–8 is a good number • Avoid hierarchy, it gets in the way of free exchange
• Create an environment for sharing • Knowledge is content-specific • Balance enquiry with advocacy	Planning • Get clear on the purpose • Consider the timing • Engage a facilitator • Get a diverse group of participants •
• Consciously move to what is possible • Focus on options • Offer insights not opinions	**Action** • Do it in time to make changes • Tell peers what you plan to do and report progress • If nothing changes you have wasted people's time
Meeting Format • Keep context to 2 hours • Let visitors take over the lead • Consider options • Give time to reflect • Present Feedback	A peer assist • Is about peers helping peers • Is usually a 2-day meeting where people share know-how, options and insights • Leads to actions which change the outcome

Appendix B
– Operations Excellence Practices

1 Use the right people and processes

- Lead and communicate effectively
- Manage asset and organizational effectiveness
- Develop and assure competency
- Raise morale and motivation
- Drive performance improvement
- Share, transfer and embed know-how
- Enhance our reputation with community

2 Cause no harm to people or the environment

- Getting HSE Right
- Manage Greenhouse Gas emissions (GHG)
- Manage water

3 Eliminate unplanned outages

- Manage production losses
- Exploit good reliability processes
- Manage integrity
- Operate equipment reliably

4 Effectively prioritize and execute planned work

- Plan, schedule and execute work
- Prepare and execute turnarounds

5 Optimize production

- Optimize plant performance
- Satisfy customers
- Exploit advanced production technology

6 Minimize cost

- Manage OPEX budget
- Manage contracted (3rd party) services
- Manage process consumable costs
- Manage spare parts and stores
- Manage energy costs and efficiency
- Manage working capital

Resources 1
– Inspirational Reading,
People and Technologies

I n compiling these resources, we wanted to avoid providing an all-inclusive library of knowledge management materials – the Internet has several of these. We have identified here the materials that you would find on our desks (or PCs) today if you came into our offices! We have included books and papers that we have *really* read and applied, the people who have inspired us, and the technologies which have made a difference; you'll find that some of the items included are referenced on the accompanying CD.

1   Setting the Context

  • Your company's annual report!

2   What is Knowledge Management?

  • This book is also available in Spanish
    (http://www.paidos.com), Mandarin and Slovenian
  • *The Knowledge-Creating Company: How Japanese Companies Create the Dynamics of Innovation*, Ikujiro Nonaka, Hirotaka Takeuchi
  • *Working Knowledge:* Thomas Davenport, Laurence Prusak
  • Prokesch, S. E. 'Unleashing the Power of Learning: An interview with British Petroleum's John Browne' *HBR* 1997, September–October

- *Performance Through Learning: Knowledge Management in Practice* Carol Gorelick, Kurt April and Nick Milton
- Knoco Ltd (http://www.knoco.co.uk). A consultancy formed by several former members of BP's knowledge management team, specializing in coaching, facilitation, training and support.

3   The Holistic Model – It's More Than the Sum of the Parts

- *Information Space: A Framework for Learning in Organisations, Institutions and Culture*, Max H. Boisot

4   Getting the Environment Right

- Argyris, C. 'Teaching Smart People How to Learn' *HBR*. 1991 May–June. pp 99–109
- *Simplicity: The New Competitive Advantage in a World of More, Better, Faster*, Bill Jensen
- *The Fifth Discipline Fieldbook: Strategies and Tools for Building a Learning Organization*, Peter Senge
- *Managing at the Speed of Change*, Daryl Conner
- *Facilitator's Guide to Participatory Decision-Making*, Sam Kaner
- *The Diary of a Change Agent*, Tony Page
- *Turning to One Another: Simple Conversations to Restore Hope to the Future*, Margaret Wheatley

5   Getting Started – Just Do It

- No resources needed – just you, and this book!

6   Connecting Sharers with Learners – Using Self-Assessment

- KM Self-Assessment tool and river diagram generator (CD)

7   Learning From Your Peers – Somebody Has Already Done It

- One page summary (CD, and see p. 300)

- *Dialogue: And the Art of Thinking Together,* William Isaacs

8 Learning Whilst Doing - Time to Reflect

- Center for Army Lessons Learned - Leader's guide to After Action Reviews. http://www.au.af.mil/au/awc/ awcgate/army/tc_25-20/guide.htm
- One page summary (CD, and see p. 301)

9 Learning After Doing - When it's All Over

- One page summary (CD, and see p. 302)

10 Finding the Right People - If Only I Knew Who

- SigmaConnect knowledge directory used in BP: http://www.sigmaconnect.com (sample page on CD)
- One page summary (see p. 303)

11 Networking and Communities of Practice

- One page summary (CD, and see p. 304)
- The community of practice for readers of *Learning to Fly*: http://www.learning-to-fly.org

12 Leveraging What We Have Learned - Capturing Knowledge

- Knoco Ltd (http://www.knoco.co.uk). A consultancy formed by several former members of BP's knowledge management team, specializing in coaching, facilitation, training and support.
- Henderson, J. C. and Sussman, S. W. (1997) 'Creating and Exploiting Knowledge for Fast-Cycle Organizational Response: The Center for Army Lessons Learned', Boston University Working Paper No 96-39.
- One page summary (CD, and see p. 305)

13 Embedding it in The Organization – Preparing To Let Go

- *The Goal: A Process of Ongoing Improvement*, Eliyahu M. Goldratt, Jeff Cox
- *The Tipping Point: How Little Things Can Make a Big Difference*, Malcolm Gladwell

14 Review of the Book – What Did We Set Out To Do?

- Let us know what you thought: contact Chris and Geoff by visiting: http://www.learning-to-fly.org

Resources 2
– One Page Resources

The pages in this section have been designed for you to re-use. Please feel free to photocopy, apply and share. They are also available electronically as downloads on the CD.

Learning From Your Peers – Someone Has Already Done It

1   *Communicate the purpose*. Peer assists work well when the purpose is clear and you communicate that purpose to participants.

2   *Share your peer assist plans with others*. Consider whether someone else has already solved the problem. They may have similar needs.

3   *Identify a facilitator* for the meeting external to the team. The role of the facilitator is to ensure that by managing the process the meeting participants reach the desired outcome.

4   *Schedule a date* for the peer assist. Ensure it is early enough to do something different with what you have learned.

5   *Invite potential participants* who have the diversity of skills, competencies and experience needed for the peer assist. Avoid 'the Usual Suspects.' It works well with six to eight people. Break up larger groups so everyone gets to voice their experience and ideas.

6   *Get clear on the desired deliverables* of the peer assist (usually options and insights), and then plan the time to achieve that.

7   *Allow time to socialize* in order to develop rapport.

8   *Allow a day and a half for the peer assist*. Schedule time to Tell, Ask, Analyse and Feedback.

9   *Create the right environment*. Spend some time creating the right environment for sharing. Plan the event to allow a balance between telling and listening.

10   *Listen for understanding* and how you might improve your own activity.

11   *Consider who else might benefit from this knowledge*, then share it with them.

12   *Commit to actions* and keep the peer assist team updated.

Learning Whilst Doing – Time to Reflect

1 *Hold the AAR immediately.* AARs are carried out immediately whilst all of the participants are still available, and their memories are fresh. Learning can then be applied right away, even on the next day.

2 *Create the right climate.* The ideal climate for an AAR to be successful is one of openness and commitment to learning. Everyone should participate in an atmosphere free from the concept of seniority or rank. AARs are learning events rather than critiques. They certainly should not be treated as personal performance evaluation.

3 *Appoint a facilitator.* The facilitator of an AAR is not there to 'have' answers, but to help the team to 'learn' answers. People must be drawn out, both for their own learning and the group's learning.

4 *Ask 'what was supposed to happen?'* The facilitator should start by dividing the event into discrete activities, each of which had (or should have had) an identifiable objective and plan of action. The discussion begins with the first activity: 'What was supposed to happen?'

5 *Ask 'what actually happened?'* This means the team must understand and agree facts about what happened. Remember, though, that the aim is to identify a problem not a culprit.

6 *Now compare the plan with reality.* The real learning begins as the team of teams compares the plan to what actually happened in reality and determines 'Why were there differences?' and 'What did we learn?' Identify and discuss successes and shortfalls. Put in place action plans to sustain the successes and to improve upon the shortfalls.

7 *Record the key points.* Recording the key elements of an AAR clarifies what happened and compares it to what was supposed to happen. It facilitates sharing of learning experiences within the team and provides the basis for a broader learning programme in the organization.

Learning After Doing – When it's All Over

1   *Call the meeting.* Hold a face-to-face meeting as soon as you can after the project ends, within weeks rather than months.

2   *Invite the right people.* The project leader needs to attend, as do key members of the project team. If a similar project is underway, then there is great value in the new project team attending.

3   *Appoint a facilitator.* Identify a facilitator who was not closely involved in the project.

4   *Revisit the objectives and deliverables of the project.* Ask 'what did we set out to do?' and 'what did we achieve?'

5   *Go through the project step by step.* Revisit the project plan and identify any deviation from plan. Where were the delays and what went ahead of schedule?

6   *Ask 'what went well?'* Ask 'what were the successful steps towards achieving your objective?' and 'what went really well in the project?' Ask a 'why?' question several times. This will get you to the root of the reason.

7   *Find out why these aspects went well, and express the learning as advice for the future.* Acknowledge feelings and press for the facts. Ask 'what repeatable, successful processes did we use?' and 'how could we ensure future projects go just as well, or even better?'

8   *Ask 'what could have gone better?'* Ask 'what were the aspects that stopped you delivering even more?' Identify the stumbling blocks and pitfalls, so they can be avoided in future by asking 'what would your advice be to future project teams, based on your experiences here?'

9   *Ensure that participants leave with their feelings acknowledged.* Ask for 'Marks out of ten' and 'What would make it a ten for you?' to access residual issues.

10 *Record the meeting.* Use quotes to express the depth of feeling. Express the recommendations as clearly, measurably and unambiguously as possible. Ensure that you circulate the write-up around the participants for comment before sharing more widely.

Finding the Right People – If Only I Knew Who

1 *Maintain a clear and distinctive vision.* Be clear about what you are trying to achieve and avoid compromise. Beware of becoming 'all things to all men' – particularly those in the HR and IT departments!

2 *Strive for personal ownership and maintenance.* Create a process whereby only the individuals concerned can create and update their entries. This will drive a far deeper sense of ownership across the population.

3 *Strike a balance between informal and formal content.* Encourage people to share non-work information about themselves in addition to valuable business information. Consider prompting for this with 'fun' questions.

4 *Support with photographs wherever possible.* Nothing is more powerful and personal than a photograph. It speaks volumes about the person, raises the interest levels of others and generates personal ownership of the content.

5 *Ensure that your product design is flexible and inclusive.* Recognize that different people relate to templates and structure in different ways. Use focus groups to test opinion.

6 *Start with a customer-facing pilot.* Critical mass is all important, so start with a group of people who have a natural need to be visible to internal customers.

7 *Deliver through local enthusiasts.* Centrally-driven push isn't always the best way to engage the workforce. Tap into local enthusiasts if possible.

8 *Use success stories as a marketing tool.* Reinforce the usefulness of the knowledge directory at every opportunity. Publicize any examples or successes widely.

9 *Encourage use, but lead by example rather than edict.* Avoid mandating the population to use the knowledge directory. People will provide better quality content if they feel that they are volunteering the information.

10 *Embed into people processes.* Look for process 'hooks' that could initiate and sustain the use of your knowledge directory (e.g. recruitment or induction).

Networking and Communities of Practice

1   *Quick wins coming from sharing what we know* across the organization. Rapid responses to queries enables the community to flourish.

2   *Provide a Web site and a discussion forum.* This is used for sharing key documents, standards, a common model, procedures and in particular the contact details of members.

3   *Determine whether the community is about* developing the capability of the individual or collectively accountable for delivering a business objective.

4   *Establish a clear, simple governing document.* Typically a community of practice would have a 'terms of reference', and a more formal network would have a set of objectives or performance contract agreed with a sponsor.

5   *Identify and refresh membership,* as people leave and join according to their changing needs. Welcome new members with a personal e-mail or telephone call.

6   *Meet face-to-face* and allow for socialization. Formal networks should aim to meet face-to-face at least once a year to establish and maintain relationships. Avoid cramming the agenda and allow plenty of time for socializing in these gatherings.

7   *Select a coordinator* who is sociable, knowledgeable and who connects people to stimulate collaboration.

8   *Delivery networks thrive on support from senior management.* Identify a sponsor to agree objectives and/or a mentor to provide assurance, coaching and resources.

9   *Consider the community as stewards of the organizations knowledge.* Expect them to keep the knowledge valid, accessible and refreshed.

Leveraging What We Have Learned – Capturing Knowledge

1 *Identify a customer for this knowledge.* Have a clear customer – current or future – in mind when considering the creation of a knowledge asset.

2 *Get clear what your knowledge asset is really about.* What is the scope of your knowledge asset? A knowledge asset needs to cover a specific area of business activity.

3 *Identify a community of practice relating to this subject.* The community will be the source of the knowledge in the first place the users of the knowledge in future, and the people who validate the knowledge in the knowledge asset.

4 *Collate any existing material upon which you can base your knowledge asset and look for general guidelines.* Provide some context so that people can understand the purpose and relevance of the knowledge asset. Are there general guidelines that you can distil out of this material?

5 *Build a checklist illustrated with examples and stories.* The checklist should tell the user of the knowledge asset:
   • 'What are the questions I need to ask myself?'
   • 'What are the steps that I need to take?'
   Illustrate it with examples, stories, pictures, models, quotes, video and audio clips if possible.

6 *Include links to people.* Create a hyperlink to the persons personal homepage or e-mail address wherever you mention them in the text. Include a list of all the people with any relationship with the content

7 *Validate the Guidelines.* Circulate the guidelines around the community again, and ask 'Do the guidelines accurately reflect your knowledge and experience?' 'Do you have anything to add?'

8 *Publish the knowledge asset.* Store the knowledge in a space where it can be accessed by its community. Often this will mean the company intranet.

9 *Initiate a feedback and ownership process.* Encourage feedback from users, so that they pick up and eliminate any invalid recommendations. Instil a sense of obligation that 'if you use it, then you should add to it'.

Index